T0346836

THINK LIKE A MARINE

'People first, then ideas, then equipment.'

John Boyd, military strategist

MARK HARDIE

THINK LIKE A MARINE

ANTICIPATE ADAPT ACHIEVE

This book is dedicated to those who serve; to the fallen, the injured and to all their families.

Publication in this form © 2021 Pitkin Publishing.

Written by Mark Hardie.

The author has asserted his moral rights.

Edited by Clare Sayer
Designed by Geoff Borin
Cover design by Dave Brown at Ape Inc. Ltd
Illustrations by Peter Liddiard

ISBN: 978-1-84165-910-7

1/21

Printed in China

Pitkin Publishing
43 Great Ormond Street
London WC1N 3HZ

Contents

INTRODUCTION

I think it's fair to say that my time as a marine was one of the most significant and important periods of my life. The Royal Marines are the UK's Commando Force and the Royal Navy's own amphibious troops. They are an elite fighting force, optimised for worldwide rapid response and are able to deal with a wide spectrum of threats and security challenges. As such, marines are rigorously trained to adapt to new circumstances in order to survive and thrive. Much is made of the incredibly demanding physical training that marines have to undergo, including endurance training, assault courses and the infamous cold weather training in the Arctic. But how much is really understood about what it is to *think* like a marine?

As a marine I learned to process new information more quickly and effectively. I made *conscious* decisions to adapt. I developed a mental framework of infinite flexibility, learning through self-reflection and curiosity. This is what I wanted to explain in the pages of this book, which is intended to give guidance to anyone who recognises that it's not enough to just survive; we need to thrive as well. The book is divided into three sections: **ANTICIPATE**, which is all about thinking ahead and being prepared; **ADAPT**, which is full of practical chapters on how to get fit and become more aware of your surroundings; and **ACHIEVE**, which explains how to turn this spirit into success, through teamwork and self-improvement.

Whether you are heading into battle, or just making your way through modern life, there are elements of marine training that are incredibly valuable and relevant. This couldn't be more true at the time of writing, as we are all now adapting to life during a global pandemic. Covid-19 has shown us that some of the ideas and institutions that we thought were unshakeable were not ready for the situation we were facing. But it also showed us that, as a nation, we had huge amounts of resourcefulness and resilience. We had to learn quickly, anticipate problems, find solutions and adapt. Every single one of us has a part to play.

Royal Marines Commando training is hard, but ultimately it is focused on turning a spark into a furnace. This spirit is held and sustained by each individual marine. To create it and then sustain and make it grow takes effort, attention and awareness. It is ignited through hard habits and stressful training. It is maintained, not by accident or luck, but by working on yourself every day. It becomes a white-hot furnace through collective endeavour. It is fuelled by a conscious choice to think independently. To choose to smile in the face of adversity. To choose to make every experience, good and bad, something you would not trade. An opportunity to learn and improve.

We need to see life now as a challenge in which the situation will continue to change and, therefore, so must we.

We need to **THINK LIKE A MARINE**.

Anticipate

We all have a built-in ability to imagine how a chosen course might play out. This mental 'time travel' means we can prepare, plan ahead and even out-think our opponents. Used in isolation, it can give us an advantage; used with careful preparation and simple planning, we can start to manipulate time to become more productive.

Think Better

Over 100 years ago, the British Royal Marines made the decision that all marines were to be taught to think for themselves, something which, up to that point, soldiers had never really been encouraged to do. They stood up straight in their intimidating uniforms in thin red lines and carried out drills designed to bring as many rifles to bear on the enemy as quickly as possible.

Wear this ➤ Do this ➤ Stand up straight
Repeat

However, in 1892, the Royal Marines introduced a new drill book, which stated: 'For the future, leaders of all ranks are to be taught to think for themselves, to act on their judgement, and to depend on their own resources. They are to be trained to accept responsibility and to bear themselves in action, not like machines but as intelligent beings, each using man's best weapons – trained intelligence and energetic thought...'

This is where it all starts, with learning to 'think better'.

MARINES WERE [and still are] DIFFERENT

As the Royal Navy's amphibious troops, marines fought on ships and on land. At sea they were sharpshooters, climbing the ship's rigging to get in a good position to take shots at the officers on the enemy ship. Why? Well, if you take out the officers, you take out the thinkers.

There were many occasions where marines fought conventionally on land, but more frequently they operated in small groups from their ship. They would often be sent ashore to gather information, protect sailors or simply explore and report back. They had to have an open mind and be ready for anything, because what they encountered was often new.

During the Napoleonic Wars, Thomas Cochrane, a British Admiral who became known in France as 'The Sea Wolf', wanted to use marines to raid the French coast. His idea was that this would create confusion, tie down French troops and so stop them fighting elsewhere. This is what marines do best; they leave their opponents wondering, 'What happened?' before striking again somewhere else.

Fast-forward to the Second World War and the aftermath of the German blitzkrieg assault on France, in which the Allies were unravelled to such an extent by the German Army that the resulting confusion and disruption led to the retreat from Dunkirk. Marines in Britain suddenly found themselves guarding ports and naval air stations because of the now very real threat of German invasion. At this point Winston Churchill called for the establishment of the Combined Operations Headquarters. This was to marshal the coastal forces of the Royal Navy and the Royal Naval Reserve and combine them with a new force of volunteers to be called 'commandos', trained to out-think and out-fight the Germans. And so it was, that in 1942 the first Royal Marines Commando was formed. They went on to serve across the globe in Burma, Italy, the Adriatic, North Africa and Western Europe. The lessons they had learned from fighting in every theatre was that this was the best way to train soldiers for the hard reality of combat, making them fit, intelligent, adaptable and independent. The commando role continues to this day.

TAKE CHARGE OF YOUR MIND

Marines don't learn how to think by reading a slogan on a card. We don't learn how to think by 'liking' something on social media. We take charge of our mind and, when we do that, we can unlock our potential and start using it properly.

Understand your mind

●

Harness its potential

●

Unlock its power

This lump of matter we call a brain is wasted sitting on a sofa playing games. We can take ourselves to the far corners of the globe – even into space – if we put our minds to it, so it's essential that we learn to understand and adapt to our environment. If we really want to understand a situation or problem more quickly than our adversaries, then we have to learn how to think, and then practise doing it.

> If you **DO** more you can **BE** more.

TRAINED THINKING

The thinking brain allows you to learn a new process and, more importantly, repeat it. Some people find it easy to focus but for others focused thinking takes effort; when people find it hard to focus, we say they have a short 'attention span'. However, the reality is that they may just be hard-wired to pay more attention to their surroundings. People who see or hear things and are always on the lookout (rather than staying focused on one thing) are using their brain just as much as the person who can sit and concentrate. We might say these people are easily distracted but it's a skill that lifeguards, paramedics and police officers all need to have – these people have the potential to be good marines.

The answer is that you need to balance both elements: if you are 'easily distracted' then you need to be better at focusing; and if you ignore all distractions you'll need to become better at paying attention to your surroundings. Believe it or not, we are designed to be able to focus **AND** listen, observe, smell, feel the wind on our face. The real skill is being able to switch between the two.

RAPID SWITCHING AND RESPONDING TO TRIGGERS

We are constantly shifting between modes, from focused to 'scattered' and back again. Everyone is different; some appear unable to focus and are easily distracted by their external environment. Others may appear distracted by their own thoughts. Focused attention takes effort and training (see page 25).

When you are distracted you are often responding to a trigger. That trigger might save your life or someone else's one day, so don't listen to the teacher who complains that you can't focus. Pay attention, by all means, but learn to listen to your scattered brain when it matters.

THE SURVIVAL INSTINCT

We all have a personal survival system: the amygdalae. These small sections of the brain are part of the limbic system, which is responsible for emotions, memory and survival instincts. In particular the amygdala responds to fear, triggering our autonomic nervous system (autonomic meaning 'self-governing'). This system senses external threats and prepares the body to react, almost like sending a distress signal. We can be taught to ignore this built-in early warning system, but it is much more useful to be curious about it. Hairs stand up on the back of the neck, we feel butterflies in the stomach and, as adrenaline is pumped round the body, the heart beats faster and we experience restless legs.

You want to run away, but as a marine you are conditioned to stand. Military drill is a way of controlling this fight-or-flight response, designed to keep soldiers on the battlefield longer than their opponents.

MENTAL READINESS

Marines are trained to be physically ready to go anywhere in the world, at any time, in any climate. But they have to be mentally ready too. There are three elements to mental readiness:

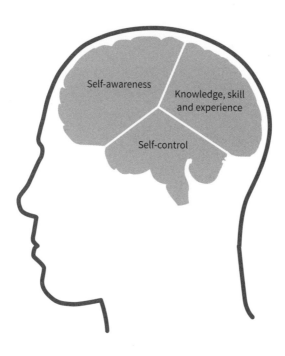

Self-awareness

Self-awareness is the ability to think clearly combined with the ability to take action. Self-awareness means accepting a bad situation for what it is, accepting that it is hard and getting through it. This is often referred to as willpower or 'strength of mind', something that marines are renowned for. For marines, this is really just about getting things done. Marines make decisions **AND** take action.

You may decide to get fit, lose weight, learn a language or take up a musical instrument. Clear thinking helps you make the right decision, but it takes courage and determination to see it through and get on with it. In this sense, courage is the ability to finish what we've started, even when it gets difficult.

Self-awareness also covers problem-solving, as this is a process that includes identifying the problem, generating solutions and picking the right one. Naming or defining the problem requires clear thinking and it can be uncomfortable, as it needs honesty. Many people like to jump straight to solving the problem as it makes them feel like they are actually doing something. Marines need to have courage to name the problem before we can find the right solution.

A decision without action achieves nothing.

Self-control

We practise self-control when we force our thinking and survival brain to work together. It is about the application of will, even under stress, to allow us to perform in the most demanding conditions.

We can complete a task, even when scared.

•

We can solve a problem under pressure.

•

We can keep running when our mind is telling us to stop.

Self-control is also about understanding our emotions; the quicker we do this, the quicker we can get control of our minds, making us more resilient. We listen to and feel emotions – and then we use them. We turn fear into bravery and suspicion into curiosity; being brave and curious helps us to make better decisions, being scared and suspicious does not.

Another aspect of self-control is what we call sequencing: breaking down a big problem or task into bite-size chunks and then putting them in the right order. When you struggle with sequencing, big tasks seem impossible. Our goals suddenly seem further away, whether it's getting to bed earlier or meeting a friend, and we end up feeling that we are not in control. Without self-control, we can become easily distracted when faced with big tasks: we hear a noise and need to investigate; we start thinking about tomorrow's worries. This is why it's often useful to think about what you really control in your life.

IN MY CONTROL	OUT OF MY CONTROL
Opinion	Environment
•	•
Intention	Illness/injury
•	•
Desire	Property
•	•
Likes	Reputation
•	•
Dislikes	Status

The reality is that you should accept that there will always be things that are out of your control. For example, no matter how much you do to influence and develop your body, you can still get injured or become ill. Reputation is what other people think of you and you have no control over that, while status is normally given and can therefore be taken away. It is far better to master the things you do control – even this will take effort and attention.

Knowledge, skill and experience

Having skills and experience is one thing but having knowledge of our strengths is what gives us confidence, while knowledge of our weaknesses gives us humility. This is what makes marines mentally ready: knowing their limitations but also being capable of learning quickly and continuously to acquire new skills. They have to be able to make their past experience useful and the ability to learn and reflect on past experience is critical and never stops. You gain knowledge, skill and experience when you recognise that you are always learning.

FLEXIBILITY

Flexibility is a critical function for revising plans and adapting in real time. Flexibility is also a key part of mental strength as it allows you to persist by changing your approach to hard work or activity rather than sticking with a bad approach.

WORKING AND LONG-TERM MEMORY

Working memory allows us to hold real-time information in our heads and process it. It's a bit like the RAM on a computer; if we overload it – for example with anxiety and fatigue or too much information – it can slow down. Long-term memory is practically unlimited in its capacity. The difference between our brain and a computer is that we don't know the limits of our long-term memory. In order for knowledge or skill to be stored in our long-term memory it must pass through our working memory. This is why we study and practise so much: folding clothes and packing kit bags uses just a tiny fraction of our working memory (particularly if we use aids such as kit lists and checklists) and will eventually be committed to our long-term memory.

PATTERN RECOGNITION

The real skill of marines is what we call pattern recognition. This is the ability to understand the true significance and dynamics of a situation with limited information. A key element to support pattern recognition is situational awareness, while seeing patterns allows us to use intuition to make faster decisions. However, it's important to balance intuition against analysis, a strategy developed by psychologist Gary Klein (see page 132).

Intuition can be unreliable:

- When a complex decision is needed.

- When there are high levels of uncertainty.

- When marines have had insufficient experience to be able to acquire expertise.

- When marines lie about their experience.

- When a marine has a mindset that they have seen it all before.

Analysis can be unreliable:

- In situations that are highly fluid and changeable.

- Under severe time constraints.

- When the goals are not clear.

- When there are too many experts in the room.

STRENGTH OF MIND

People talk about mental toughness and resilience all the time – that we don't have enough of it, or that one generation is stronger than another. One thing is for sure: your mind is only as strong as your life needs it to be.

Choose an
easy life and you will
only ever be comfortable
with easy things.

Choose a challenge and
you will build a mind that
is ready for a challenge.

Marines choose a challenging life and they develop the mind they need for that life. It is strong out of necessity.

DISCIPLINE LEADS TO SELF-DISCIPLINE

For a new recruit the first 12 weeks or 90 days feels like it is all too much, too fast. There is too much to do, too many inspections and checks. Our brains have too much to take in; we have less time to sleep. In reality it is all small, basic stuff. Many give up at this stage because they've lost sight of the bigger goal. It takes time for you to learn to take control of yourself and your belongings.

We conduct inspections to make sure that people are keeping up, that they are okay, that they are sleeping properly and looking after their kit. Marines understand that this discipline is not designed to harass them, but to keep them alive by making them better than their opponents. A good marine understands that discipline is about learning, not punishment. Parenting expert and author Barbara Coloroso explains that good discipline will:

Show them what they have done wrong.

•

Give them ownership of the problem.

•

Help them find ways to solve problems.

•

Leave their dignity intact.

We want to develop self-discipline because we need to trust people to maintain standards when they are operating independently. Over time, what took you three hours will take you 20 minutes or less. This is what makes us ready.

Be Prepared

We can be ready for anything when we are prepared in mind and body and have the right kit for the job. Getting your kit ready is down to what we call personal administration or *personal admin*. There are two essential elements needed to reach a high level of personal admin: *thinking* about the thing you need to do and *doing* the thing you need to do.

Thinking (T) x Doing (D) = Personal Admin (PA)

The second part of this equation, doing the work required, is at risk from two disruptive factors: procrastination and distraction.

PROCRASTINATION

Procrastination stops us from even starting a task in the first place. It is often the biggest obstacle to achieving the simplest of goals. Procrastination can undermine all of our good thinking in a heartbeat and makes any effort at reducing distraction completely irrelevant. Procrastination is so dangerous that it warrants a negative 'doing' score on the equation:

$$T\ (15)\ x\ D\ (-5) = PA\ (-75)$$

When we think about a task we are not looking forward to, it activates the pain centre of the brain, which can stop us from even starting.

Time and task

The best technique for dealing with procrastination is a simple time management method known as the Pomodoro Technique, which was developed by Francesco Cirillo in the late 1980s. It is a disciplined and focused intervention that applies time to the task at hand.

Reduce all distractions.

•

Set a timer for 25 minutes.

•

Start the task and focus as hard as you can. Don't switch between tasks. When you switch your attention, you waste mental energy and both tasks will suffer.

•

When the timer goes off, reward yourself with a break.

•

Repeat up to three more times before taking a longer break.

DISTRACTION

Distraction can interrupt us when we have started the task itself, so reducing distractions will allow you to get more things done. Even something as simple as having an untidy desk can become a distraction – if you are wasting time trying to find something you'll become frustrated and less effective at the task.

In the modern world we are more distracted than ever because so many of us are glued to a smartphone. In many ways these make our lives much easier, but you need to be able to take control of it and make it work for you. Here are some tips to help you reduce the distraction from your mobile phone.

Turn off all alerts

No alerts mean that you control your attention to your phone, rather than your phone controlling you. Tell yourself that whatever is happening is happening anyway; you knowing about it won't affect the outcome.

Decide how you can be contacted

We can be contacted in so many ways these days: phone calls, emails, texts, WhatsApp. Set an auto-response that says 'If this is urgent, call me.' Then when someone calls you, you'll know it's probably urgent.

Don't take your phone to bed

A bed is where you should switch off gadgets and shift focus. If you are using your phone in bed you will become distracted by it. In addition, the blue light emitted by smartphone screens has been shown to have a detrimental effect on sleep. If you need an alarm clock, get an alarm clock. Very few people are doing work so important that they need a phone by the bed.

Don't pick up your phone first thing in the morning

Just don't.

Make social media harder to access

This constant stream of information from social media on your phone is making you dance like a puppet. If you have to use social media, try setting your own limits.

Reduce your contacts

Not just in your contacts/address book, but across social media, whether it's Facebook, Instagram or LinkedIn.

Set your phone to 'do not disturb'

Some things are not worth your attention.

Go 'old school'

Write a letter, buy a magazine, listen to the radio. By not relying so heavily on your phone you will become less likely to be distracted by it.

PERFORMANCE AIDS

There are simple performance aids we can use to help maintain a basic level of focused thinking, especially under stress. A performance aid is a tool that gives some structure to our thinking.

Follow this simple planning process, using six key question starters (think of the six honest serving men in Rudyard Kipling's poem 'The Elephant's Child').

WHAT?
Identify the problem you are trying to solve.
•
WHY?
What does success look like?
•
WHEN?
Set a deadline and stick to it.
•
HOW?
Identify specific tasks that must be done.
•
WHERE?
Identify the required spaces.
•
WHO?
Who else is required?

Checklists

We use checklists to aid our working memory as they help us make sure we have everything we need, even if we are in a rush, or are tired, angry or late. Try writing these checklists on cards, and think about making separate cards for different tasks. Whatever the size or scale of the task or problem ahead of you, using checklists will improve your ability to sequence (see page 17).

LEAVING THE HOUSE

Phone ✓

Cash ✓

Keys ✓

Travel card ✓

Check door ✓

Learn what you can control

When faced with a problem or task that appears difficult or challenging, it's essential to break the issues down as follows:

In my control / facts / certain

_____

_____

_____

_____

_____

_____

Outside of my control / speculation / uncertain

_____

_____

_____

_____

_____

Once you have done this you'll realise that the solution – the one that you can rely on – can only be formed from the elements in your control.

CREATE YOUR OWN
FEEDBACK LOOP

A feedback loop is a biological occurrence that allows living organisms to maintain homeostasis, or a constant, ideal state. It's a term that is increasingly used as an effective management tool to help people change their behaviour, the idea being that if you provide information about people's actions, they can assess how that affects the situation and are given the opportunity to change those actions, pushing them towards better outcomes.

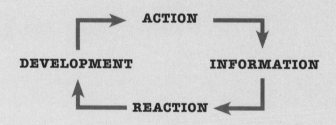

ACTION

DEVELOPMENT   INFORMATION

REACTION

Start creating a personal mental model that works for you. For example: Start asking, 'Am I ready?' Run through an essential kit 'scan' – feet to head (shoes, clothes, cash, keys, passport). Break down the tasks that need to be done into a logical sequence. Use a list if necessary. Make the tasks as simple as possible. Change your environment to eliminate distractions and procrastinations. If it is too noisy, wear headphones; too dark, use a torch. Work out what works and what doesn't and use this information next time.

Practise, Practise, Practise

Part of marine training is about getting better at simple daily routines. These routines are small repeatable actions (habits or drills) that eventually become automatic. It takes a lot of focused thinking to reach a good standard, but after three months it will come naturally; that's because creating new habits that are automatic takes about 90 days, coincidentally the length of time of most basic military training.

START WITH THE BASICS

The definition of the adjective 'basic' is as follows: 'forming an essential foundation or starting point; fundamental'. For a marine this essentially means cleaning.

Cleaning and ironing clothes

•

Cleaning shoes

•

Cleaning yourself

•

Cleaning your bed space

Folding clothes and showering properly is not hard (unlike boarding a ship in the dark or crossing a surf beach). The tasks themselves are very simple, but here is where we build the connections that help us to learn the harder stuff later. The connections that link the process with the outcome are strengthened.

TAKE CHARGE

We need to be better at taking charge and looking after ourselves and it is our responsibility to make this happen. If we can't master this then we are limiting our ability to tackle the harder things when it really does matter. The temptation to go back to old habits will be ever present. We can easily choose the wrong path over the right one – it might even get us more time on the sofa. But we can safely say that we will struggle further down the line, and then we'll have to ask ourselves 'Why is this so hard?'

AUTOMATIC

Learning these techniques will take some focused thinking and daily practice. They become simple drills that we repeat and complete every day. Repetition increases the tempo at which we complete each task – but crucially, doing things faster should never mean cutting corners. Everything counts.

This is about creating your own autopilot: being on autopilot allows you to get things done while thinking about other things. It is the foundation of constructive concurrent activity. If folding a shirt takes too much thinking, you'll be in trouble when you're faced with a really tricky problem.

'Make it basic to make it easy.'

Good habits or drills take organisation. Define what you want to do and pair it with obvious actions to start the activity, as well as a reward for when it is done. Make it a ritual.

RIG YOUR ENVIRONMENT

By organising your belongings, you are rigging your environment to work for you. Marines reduce the size of their environment to their bed space and locker. When they are in the field, they reduce it to their pockets, pouches and pack.

FIND A BUDDY

It's not just your physical environment that influences your behaviour, it is also the people around you. Motivation is contagious. The buddy system makes you accountable. If you've made a commitment to another person or group, you're more likely to stick with it.

START SMALL

Habits build upon themselves. Pick a part of your room or home to organise, so that it works better for you. A simple starting point for a good habit is to put a small tray near your front door and make sure you always leave your keys, cash and phone on this tray. Whenever you need to prepare to leave the house, the stuff you need will be on the tray. When you arrive home again, put it on the tray.

Add to these items to create what is often referred to as 'everyday carry' or EDC items and always keep your EDC in the same place. Pocket items that you might find useful when you are away from home include:

Small torch

•

Small pocket or multitool

•

Pen and notebook

•

Watch

BE STRICT WITH YOURSELF AND TOLERANT OF OTHERS

There will be times when you fail, often at the point just before you start to improve or just before everything 'falls into place'. The key is to not be too easy on yourself: if you create excuses, then you won't be taking responsibility for yourself; if you are too hard on yourself ('I'm no good, I'll never be able to do this.'), then you'll be creating a narrative that is just not true. You are not thinking clearly.

You need to accept that it is hard and just keep going. Once you have started to master the small things in life and make them count, you may see that others around you have not reached the same standard. Standards matter, but if someone needs your help, offer it.

THE KIT MUSTER

Maintaining good routines and habits wastes less time. The best way to get to this point is to 'muster' all of your belongings, or carry out what is called a kit muster. Marines (and most other military personnel) have to practise this over and over again throughout basic training. This is to ensure that everyone is maintaining the same high standards, whatever the conditions. Although this may seem time-consuming and laborious, it is worth the effort. We could call this tidying up, but in fact we are getting our stuff 'squared away' – a nautical term for aligning sails at right angles.

Start big and slow

Find a clear spot and lay out your clothes and shoes and any other items from your wardrobe. Start to organise everything into categories:

Small daily items
(underwear, socks)

Daily winter work items
(shirts, tops, bottoms)

Going out summer items
(shirts, tops, bottoms)

Daily accessories

Daily spring/autumn work items
(shirts, tops, bottoms)

Going out winter items
(shirts, tops, bottoms)

Activity footwear

Daily summer work items
(shirts, tops, bottoms)

Sportswear
(underwear, socks, t-shirts, shorts)

Special occasion footwear

Luggage
(weekend, holiday)

Daily footwear

Special occasion accessories

When you lay out all of your kit in order, you can see what you need less of, and what you need more of, in a way that cupboards and drawers don't allow. Go through it all and work out whether there are any items you don't need; put these to one side. The next step is to allocate spaces in your drawers and cupboards based on frequency of use. Now you are ready to fold or hang items in such a way that they will fit where they are going and be ready at hand.

Folding shirts and trousers

Whether you are tidying things away in your cupboards and drawers or packing clothes for a trip away, it helps to keep things organised if you fold items to the same size. Here's how it's done, using a magazine (or something of similar A4 size).

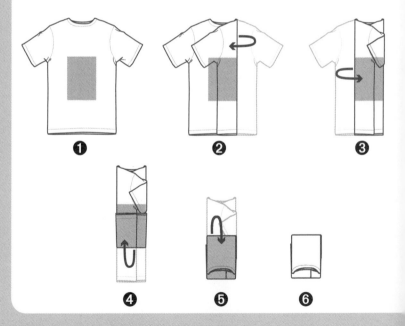

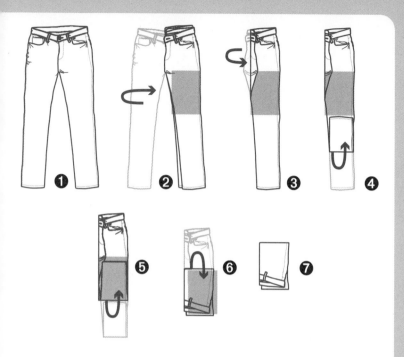

Rolling socks so they 'smile'

This is an easy way to create space in your drawers.

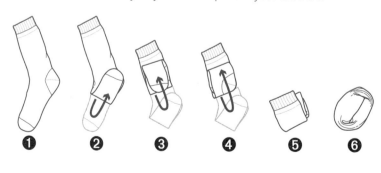

START TOMORROW AT THE END OF TODAY

This is a simple technique that will help you start the day better. You will gain valuable time in the morning if you choose your clothes the night before.

Lay out the clothes and things you need for tomorrow in a kit muster. If you have more than one activity requiring different clothes, lay them all out.

•

Check everything is clean and serviceable and carry out any repairs if needed.

•

If your shirt needs ironing, do it now.

•

Pack your kit.

•

Lay the table for breakfast.

•

Prepare the coffee machine, etc.

•

Go to bed.

START TODAY PROPERLY

1 Get up.

2 Make your bed. This means that you start your day with a simple task complete, and also have a welcoming bed ready for you at the end of the day. Traditionally marines' beds use sheets and blankets – the colder the weather, the more blankets are issued. Fitted sheets are not supplied, so marines are taught hospital corners. During inspections you could tell who was on top of their routines by how well made their bed was.

3 Clean yourself. Marines wash their entire body from head to toe every morning, after any physical activity or exercise and before bed. This is especially important on board ship or in the field.

4 Put on your socks properly. This is critical – creases or folds in the wrong place can lead to blisters.

5 Leave the house on time with your everyday carry.

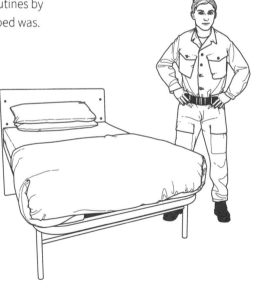

PACKING

Good packing has to start with a kit list. Look at the following example, for a two-day overnight work trip:

Travel suit (made from material that is more crease-resistant)	**Running shorts and shoes**
2 x smart shirts	**Pyjama bottoms**
1 x casual shirt	**Small travel pillow**
1 x pair of jeans + belt	**Laundry bag**
1 x smart shoes	**Wash bag**
1 x casual shoes	**Earplugs**
2 x t-shirts	**2 x handkerchiefs**
Underwear	**Travel toiletries** (hotel rooms can be unpredictable)

Once you have this you can carry out a kit muster for the trip. Lay everything out and then ruthlessly remove items you don't need. Fold each item using your magazine (see page 38), but this time fold everything in half again. Carrying out a kit muster means we can pick the right sized bag for the right amount of kit.

When it comes to the packing, put heavier items in first. Fill dead space (with socks or underwear, for example) and make sure you can easily access daily items if you are living out of the bag for the duration of your trip.

APPLICATION REQUIRES
SKILL AND EFFORT

In order to be skilled at something you need to start with good technique; good technique converts potential into performance. When you have mastered a good technique for folding a shirt, you can apply that technique to improve your packing. Better performance leads to increased confidence; confidence in your ability means that you are willing to increase the load and learn harder things. You can aim higher.

You have done the basic work required to build a strong foundation. Building new habits is not hard; shaking old ones is. Every now and again your mind will suggest going back to a bad habit because you are tired or under pressure. Stop and think: keep it big, basic and simple. Remember, drills are habits and we improve every time we do the drill.

Building new habits is not hard; shaking old ones is.

Adapt

When faced with any new challenge we have a choice: to react and let the challenge control us, or to act and take control ourselves. This is why marines train their minds as well as their bodies. This flexibility of thought creates adaptability. By paying attention to our surroundings we create the foundation to adapt to any situation through conscious daily effort.

Get Fit

A marine is fit because the job demands it. Because the Marines historically operated on ships at sea as well as on land, they needed to be useful in both environments. Imagine being told to climb the rigging of a ship at sea carrying weapons and 10kg of equipment on your back. There simply isn't the option of saying, 'Sorry, I can't do that.' Or if you're sent to explore a coastline, paddle a small boat to the shore and swim the final stages through the surf to protect the boat: 'Sorry, I can't swim' just won't cut it. With that one statement you move from being someone useful to someone useless.

But if that was your job, you'd make sure that you were fit enough to be useful. Getting up the rigging or swimming to the shore is just the commute to work for a marine. If you're not physically fit, you can't adapt and there's no point being fit if you can't be useful with it.

YOUR BODY IS ADAPTABLE

Your body is amazing. It will adapt to your environment in amazing ways. Get up and move every day and you will get the body you need for that life. But sit on a sofa and feed your body cake every day and it will adapt to sitting on a sofa and eating cake. You will get the body you need for the life you have chosen.

FITNESS = USEFULNESS

Fitness is about how prepared you are for physical work. For marines it is not about aesthetics, it is about being useful and that means having a high level of general fitness based on strength, endurance and mobility. The specific technical skills that you see in the world of athletes and sports personalities don't have the same value for marines; a table tennis player may be at the top of his or her game but those skills are not necessarily useful or transferable. A superstar footballer may be a fantastic goal-scorer but if he can't work as part of a team he is useless.

> 'You are fit if you can adapt to the demands of your environment with ease and imagination.'
>
> Edwin Checkley, *A Natural Method of Physical Training*, 2012, Forgotten Books.

THREE TYPES OF CHALLENGE

Fitness is also about challenging yourself and, in many cases, having fun. There are three types of challenge in the Marines.

Type 1 This is what we know as real fun. It's the kind of activity we look forward to and can be enjoyed by anyone, such as playing sports, going for a lovely bike ride or playing beach volleyball.

Type 2 This is only fun on reflection and is more about facing adversity, usually as a result of extreme climate or weather conditions, such as those found in the desert, the jungle or the Arctic. You may not be enjoying it at the time, and it's probably quite physically demanding, but you know why you want to do it.

Type 3 There will be times in our lives when we face more difficult challenges, such as serious injury, illness or bereavement. Yet we need to face them with as much cheerfulness and enthusiasm as we can muster. We need to accept the brutal facts of the situation and not turn away from them. We need to take productive action and accept that the situation will continue to change and, therefore, so must we. We need to know that we will prevail but accept that it could take many months – even years – for us to recover and grow from the experience.

For the average person, simply trying to get fit can feel like a Type 3 challenge. This is often because people start too hard, too fast and struggle right from the start.

Your heart rate is a good indicator of which type of challenge you are undertaking. Anything where the heart rate is above 175 bpm is not fun for most people. Marines spend a lot of time in this space. It is rarely comfortable, but experiencing it is necessary.

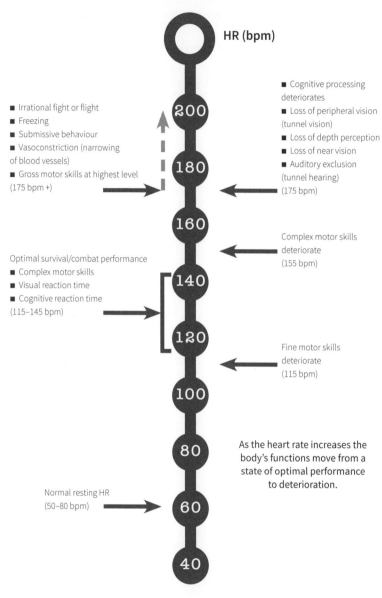

HR (bpm)

■ Cognitive processing deteriorates
■ Loss of peripheral vision (tunnel vision)
■ Loss of depth perception
■ Loss of near vision
■ Auditory exclusion (tunnel hearing)
(175 bpm)

200

■ Irrational fight or flight
■ Freezing
■ Submissive behaviour
■ Vasoconstriction (narrowing of blood vessels)
■ Gross motor skills at highest level (175 bpm +)

180

160

Complex motor skills deteriorate
(155 bpm)

Optimal survival/combat performance
■ Complex motor skills
■ Visual reaction time
■ Cognitive reaction time
(115–145 bpm)

140

120

Fine motor skills deteriorate
(115 bpm)

100

80

As the heart rate increases the body's functions move from a state of optimal performance to deterioration.

Normal resting HR
(50–80 bpm)

60

40

START FROM THE GROUND UP

The best way to start a fitness programme from a less active lifestyle is to start with the feet. Your feet play an absolutely critical role in how you control your body and how you react. The foot has 26 bones, 33 joints, 19 muscles and 107 ligaments. It also contains thousands of small nerves that are sensitive to every subtle movement we make. The feet form and support our relationship with gravity, from walking and running to jumping and balancing. Your feet have small nerve receptors sensitive to texture, vibration, pressure and skin stretch. Feet can respond quickly and even anticipate action.

As well as looking after your feet by wearing well-fitting shoes, walking barefoot whenever possible and having the occasional foot massage, there are a number of strengthening exercises you can do.

Whenever you walk make sure your feet are pointing straight ahead.

•

Challenge yourself by trying to pick up marbles with your toes.

•

Begin the day by rolling your foot over a spiky massage or foam roller ball.

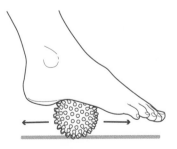

At certain points in the day, try lifting and spreading your toes and holding for 30 seconds. This will help you develop stronger toe flexors.

●

Consider investing in a stability disc or slant board – these pieces of equipment are great for improving balance and developing the neural pathways connected to movement.

●

Drill is ballroom dancing for marines

Having a good connection to the ground increases your reaction times as any activity that demands quick reactions relies on correct foot placement. You may see marines carrying out drill on a parade square and think it is an old-fashioned waste of time that has no place in a modern military. Yet some people struggle with the simple coordination required to walk around smartly. Every period on the drill square is building the neural pathways between the feet and the brain, thereby increasing the response and reaction times. It does not mean that no thought is required, just that less thought is required because the movements become automatic as a result of practice and repetition. When taught well, basic drill movements build a strong foundation for other more complex skills. Ballroom dancing takes the same principle: it's all about foot placement and practice leading to automatic and quick responses.

THE 10 KEY FITNESS SKILLS
FOR A MARINE

Drill used to be all it took to train a soldier. That all changed when the Boer War (1899–1902) forced the British Army to modify its approach. Out went the red coats and standing up straight; in came fieldcraft, khaki uniforms and taking cover. Meanwhile, in France this new approach gained traction from their own experience in the Franco-Prussian war when a French officer called Georges Hébert developed his 'Natural Method' of training. Hébert was one of the first to introduce obstacle courses to develop the sort of fitness that was useful for a soldier. The tragedy of the First World War is that the French and British failed to continue this approach after defeating Germany. The problem of the Second World War is that, between the wars, the Germans did. Hébert broke down his natural method of training into three blocks totalling 10 skills:

Pursuit	Escape	Attack
Walk	Climb	Throw
Run	Balance	Lift
Crawl	Jump	Fight
	Swim	

The interesting thing about these skills is that most of them are things that we instinctively practise as children – just look around any park or school playground. Each of these skills requires effort and improving these skills will improve physical fitness, meaning that you are more able to adapt. We need to start small and gradually build up so that the body is forced to adapt to increasing levels of stress or tension (this is often referred to as progressive overload). Let's look at how to improve strength and fitness so that we can acquire and develop these key skills.

This is where the concept of strength-to-muscle-mass ratio comes in; it is not about increasing muscle or 'bulk' but about producing large amounts of strength in tightly packed groups of muscles. There are two workouts that we need to look at. The first is a slow lifting workout, or what is sometimes called a 'push–pull' workout.

Perform 15–20 minutes of slow, controlled lifting exercises, including:

- **Upper-body push**
(overhead press, chest press)

- **Upper-body pull**
(bent or upright rows, pull-ups)

- **Lower-body push**
(leg press, squats)

- **Lower-body pull**
(dead lifts)

The second workout is a high-intensity circuit programme, often called the 7-minute workout. Designed by two researchers from the Human Performance Institute in Orlando, Florida, its aim is to improve and maintain strength and muscle in as little time as possible. Each of the 12 exercises should be done hard for 30 seconds, with a 10-second rest between each one; from there aim to do the exercises for 2 minutes each, with a 30-second rest between each one.

Jumping jacks (or burpees)

Wall sits

Push-ups

Abdominal crunches

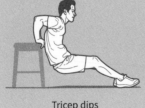

Tricep dips

Squats (or squat jumps)

Plank

Step-ups

Lunge (or lunge jumps)

Jump rope
(or high knees/running in place)

Push-ups with rotation

Side planks

The great things about these exercises is that they require minimal kit or equipment, can be done alone or with a buddy and are free (no need to join a gym), although if you are new to these types of exercises you may find a good gym instructor or personal trainer helpful. There are also any number of good online resources, including YouTube videos and apps to help you with your form. Now let's return to the 10 key skills.

Pursuit: Walk

Walking is a gift and anyone who is able to walk should be grateful for it every day. We used to walk everywhere – ancient footpaths criss-cross the country connecting towns and villages. If you are neither ill nor injured, walking should not intimidate you. We are also capable of walking with weight on our backs. The average human should be able to walk 3 mph over hill and dale, whereas a marine carrying 50 kg can average 2.5 mph in the mountains. And in the Second World War a commando had to be able to march the following in full kit:

| 1hr | 2hrs | 4.5hrs | 8hrs | 14hrs |
| 5 miles | 9 miles | 15 miles | 25 miles | 35 miles |

And still be ready to fight after 2 hours' rest...*

---

* James Dunning, *It Had to be Tough*, 2012, Frontline Books.

Pursuit: Run

Humans are designed to run: we have large muscles in our legs and backsides, long Achilles tendons, fatigue-resistant slow-twitch muscles and the ability in the leg muscles to use oxygen as fuel when running. We even have a ligament at the base of the skull that we share with other species that run (dogs and horses) that stops the head moving too much when we run. These are adaptations that helped humans survive. Our body is designed to cover distance on foot every day and it's disheartening that so many of us don't use our bodies for what they were designed for. Marines are lucky; running is part of the job. Running is free.

The best way to start running and make it part of your life is to 'slow down to speed up'. Start running at a slow pace where you can breathe through your nose. If you feel the need to breathe through your mouth while running at this pace, then slow down to a walk. The aim is to be able to run at a pace of 9 minutes per mile while breathing through your nose and having a conversation. If you can't talk you are either not fit enough or are running too fast. To get to this sort of speed from zero running will take time and effort as you will be running very slowly at the start, but your body will adapt. You will get stronger and fitter.

Pursuit: Crawl

Few people nowadays have any need to crawl, but it is a great whole-body workout. Crawling is an essential part of marine fitness and the current trend for obstacle course racing may have jump-started a trend for more crawling as part of a training session. For marines there are two crucial elements to add to the crawl: getting down and getting up again quickly. So, to master the crawl we need to get better at another favourite exercise, the burpee. For most people these are a Type 3 challenge (see page 48) and there are few exercises that are as demanding – or effective. The movement is done in four steps: begin in standing, move down into a squat, kick your feet back into a plank position and extend your arms, then immediately jump back to a squat before jumping up to standing.

Escape: Climb

Alex Honnold is living proof of how humans adapt to the demands of their environment with ease and imagination. In the film *Free Solo* he climbs El Capitan in Yosemite with no ropes or equipment in a little over 4 hours, his body and mind working in perfect harmony on a climb of over 3,000 feet.

Climbing is one of the best activities to combine physical exercise with brain function and technical skill. Basic climbing, where the hand and foot holds are big, is within the grasp of any reasonably fit person. Start adding height, wind and exposure and it gets harder. You become activated and simple moves suddenly become extremely complex. To become good at climbing requires good technique and relevant skills in rope-work and protection.

Escape: Balance, Jump

Your feet are essential for good balance and jumping. Obstacles are part of a marine's life. To be useful we need to be able to get from one point to another, regardless of what might be in the way. Whilst Hébert tied it to escaping (see page 52), for commandos, being able to balance and jump is also about successful infiltration, getting to a position that our opponents think is impossible.

Escape: Swim

Swimming is one of the best forms of exercise but to swim well takes good technique and good breathing; without these, swimming quickly becomes exhausting. Marines need to be confident in the water and every marine has to be able to swim with equipment on.

There are two basic situations where being able to swim is important: to save your own life or to save someone else's. Many people can swim reasonably well but this ability alone does not guarantee that you will be able to do either of these in an emergency. Here is the RNLI advice for what to do if you enter the water unexpectedly:

- Take a minute. The initial effects of being in cold water pass in less than a minute so don't try to swim straight away.
- Relax and float on your back to catch your breath and then steady your breathing. Try to get hold of something that will help you float.
- Keep calm, then call for help or swim to safety if you're able.

Attack: Throw, Lift, Fight

To fight with skill takes discipline, self-awareness and self-control. People who fight without those elements hurt others and – frequently – themselves. Martial arts and other combat sports are an excellent way to enhance fitness and develop mental strength. They also improve body awareness and boost brain function.

Western-style boxing combines breathing with footwork and technical skill – the ability to control your thinking and your activation when being hit is demanding, and remembering to breathe when punching is not as easy as you might think. Regaining composure between rounds takes discipline and getting back in the ring takes courage. It is a mix of physical, technical and mental focus that demand adaptation over time. Take up boxing and you will see and feel your reaction times improve.

Brazilian jiu-jitsu is another route to improving physical, technical and mental focus. It is an environment where regular training forces adaptation on the body through necessary increases in strength and mobility. According to a serving Royal Marine and BJJ practitioner: 'BJJ offers many lessons to its students: physically of course, but also mentally and philosophically. Physically it develops fitness, self-defence, self-awareness and confidence. It helps you understand body position, balance and mechanics. Mentally it teaches you to overcome fear and panic from pain or chokes and to manage your breathing under stress. There is a discipline involved in continued training – even when you don't feel up to it. Finally the philosophical lessons are about humility and tolerance. The golden rule is to treat others as you would expect to be treated. Work with what you are given rather than what you want to get. The right technique at the wrong time is the wrong technique – and this applies equally to how you approach situations and problems in life.'

All marines are taught unarmed close-quarters combat skills. While this training includes technical locks, holds and strikes, it also covers conflict management, from escalation to de-escalation. Avoiding a confrontation is better for everyone, but if you have to fight, then make sure you can win. Learning how to fight properly gives you a quiet confidence based on skill, knowledge and, occasionally, hard experience.

EXERCISE IMPROVES THE BRAIN

Physical exercise is accompanied by increased brain volume in humans. Exercise is also directly linked to better memory performance, while physical fitness in children is associated with better cognitive performance and larger brain structures. Exercise benefits the functions shown below – having all three will enhance your performance.

Cognitive function
(being mentally ready)

•

Technical function
(being able to apply the skills we have learned and practised)

•

Physical function
(being physically capable)

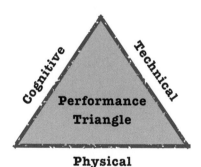

Research has also shown that different types of physical exercise can have quite specific mental benefits, from boosting your memory to improving your creativity or concentration. Take a look at the diagram overleaf to see how different activities can affect the brain.

How different activities can affect the brain

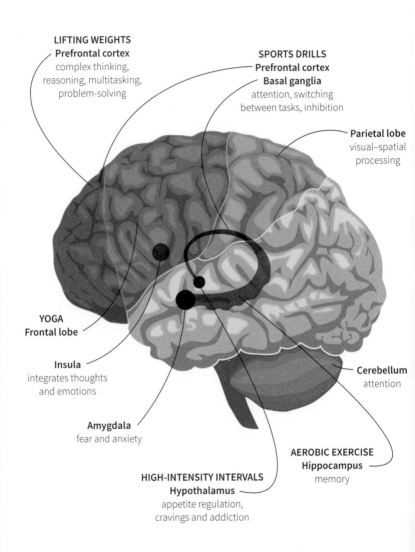

LIFTING WEIGHTS
Prefrontal cortex
complex thinking,
reasoning, multitasking,
problem-solving

SPORTS DRILLS
Prefrontal cortex
Basal ganglia
attention, switching
between tasks, inhibition

Parietal lobe
visual–spatial
processing

YOGA
Frontal lobe

Insula
integrates thoughts
and emotions

Cerebellum
attention

Amygdala
fear and anxiety

AEROBIC EXERCISE
Hippocampus
memory

HIGH-INTENSITY INTERVALS
Hypothalamus
appetite regulation,
cravings and addiction

STRESS, FEAR AND HOW TO DEAL WITH IT

The mind–body connection is real. We can and should strengthen it because part of thinking like a marine is developing a bias for action, a willingness to learn about a situation as quickly as possible and take appropriate action. You need to control the situation, not let the situation control you. Action, not reaction.

When something triggers our fear response, adrenaline pumps through our veins and the hairs on the back of the neck stand up. Fear protects us; it kept our ancestors vigilant and helped them detect and avoid physical threats. But fear can also hijack us, keeping us from performing at our peak. When we are put into difficult or stressful situations the internal thoughts can activate the body. If we feel it in our shoulders, then we may be experiencing the 'fight' response – our fear becomes confrontation. If we feel it in our legs, we are experiencing the 'flight' response – our fear becomes avoidance. If we feel it in our stomach, we want to 'freeze' – our fear becomes the hope that this will pass if we do nothing.

Here are some ways to deal with situations so that you start the task in front of you with more control.

Plant your feet

Finding your breath in stressful situations can be difficult; finding your feet is not. Planting your feet creates a contact point that you can apply focused thought to.* A contact point is the physical sensation of contact between you and your surroundings.

Stand up and position your feet flat on the ground, about shoulder width apart. Now turn your knees slightly outwards. You will notice that you appear to 'stick' to the ground. Marines get into the habit of doing this before almost every activity, whether it's climbing, jumping out of a helicopter or engaging in close-quarters combat, but it can be beneficial for anyone starting any activity, whether it's going for a run, doing Pilates or lifting weights.

Learn to breathe properly

Focus on your feet on the ground and continue to breathe through your nose. Proper breathing begins with the belly. When you breathe through your mouth you'll notice that the top of your chest expands first. What this means is that you are not making best use of your lungs and you will soon feel fatigued. Proper breathing is done through the nose, starting in the belly and filling your lungs from the bottom. It should be calm, quiet and take little thought. When you breathe through your nose you are creating the right conditions in your body for oxygen to be transferred to your muscles. Your muscles will get the amount of oxygen they need for what you are using them for. Breathe through your mouth and you become inefficient.

*Elizabeth A. Stanley, PhD, *Widen the Window*, 2019, Yellow Kite.

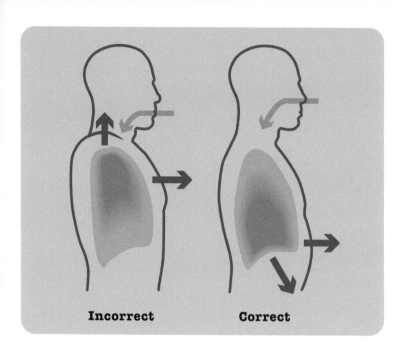

| Incorrect | Correct |

Use your breathing to control your mind

Your nervous system is made up of two parts: voluntary – the part that allows you to make a cup of tea and drink it – and involuntary – everything that happens inside your body when you drink the tea that you don't have to think about. Your beating heart and your breathing lungs are part of your involuntary nervous system, but by controlling your breathing you can create a bridge between voluntary and involuntary.

The more you practise planting your feet and breathing, the stronger the neural pathway will become. This means that you will be able to regain control of a situation faster and turn the activation or stress to your advantage. You will be able to force calm. When taking part in an activity that requires optimum performance, you should be activated and breathing through your nose. When you are running for your life you will find that you will be breathing through your mouth.

STRESSED BREATHING	CONSCIOUS BREATHING
Through the mouth	Through the nose
•	•
Chest heaving	Diaphragm and belly
•	•
Fast and tense	Slow and relaxed
•	•
Irregular	Rhythmic
•	•
Noisy and big	Quiet and reduced

Upper chest breathing is normally related to the fight/flight response and may cause reduced oxygen uptake. Taking deep breaths does help control your stress response but only if it is through the nose, abdominal, gentle and quiet. Taking big breaths through the mouth will not help you take control.

Make stress your friend

When thinking about stress it's important to know the difference between 'stressors' and 'stress'. Stressors are internal or external events that we perceive as challenging or threatening. These can be acute (e.g., a major traumatic event, or something that is immediately overwhelming or with a seemingly impossible time scale) or chronic (e.g., a low-grade situation that builds over time, slowly depleting resources and reserves). Stress is the physical and psychological response to a stressor and can be defined as 'everything that forces an organism to adapt to a new situation'. The stress response can be mobilised as a response to a genuine threat or in expectation of a threat. Just thinking about something can activate the stress response. Marines have to learn to adapt so that when they appraise the stressor, the body and mind is activated to respond in a way that is positive.

COLD WATER IMMERSION AS A WAY OF ADAPTING TO STRESS

Cold water immersion is an essential part of marine training, designed to help Royal Marines recognise and reduce the risks of cold shock: a physical response to being immersed in cold water that can incapacitate and even kill.

When you get into cold water you experience the initial gasp, rapid breathing through the mouth and increased heart rate (see heart rate chart on page 49) and blood pressure. Your body starts to adapt in two ways: insulative adaptation and hypothermic adaptation. Insulative adaptation means that the vessels supplying blood to the skin are reduced in size, limiting blood flow to the surface of the skin (vasoconstriction); repeated exposure to cold water may stimulate a quicker vasoconstrictor response. This will ensure that more of the heat in the blood supply is moved to the deep tissues of the body, leaving the skin, hands and feet to cool to a greater extent, but insulating the core from cooling.

Shivering is stimulated to increase deep body temperature when a reduction in deep body temperature occurs. It works by involuntary contractions of the muscles to generate heat and also makes movements like swimming difficult to coordinate. The hypothermic adaptation reduces the amount of shivering that occurs as the deep body temperature is reduced. Repeated bouts of cold-water immersion will reduce the shivering response – this has the effect of enabling the swimmer to coordinate movement, but at the expense of greater deep body cooling compared to someone who is shivering.

Research has shown that as few as five or six 3-minute immersions can have the effect of halving the cold shock response. However, those going through this training must listen to their body; if they start to shiver, it's time to get out of the water and start the rewarming process.

Once you exit the water, your body will continue to cool for 20–30 minutes, which is why warming up immediately is vital to prevent clinical hypothermia. This means drying off and removing wet clothes as soon as possible, dressing in dry warm clothes (including a hat, gloves and thick socks), having a warm drink and shivering.

Sharpen Your Instincts

There is no doubt that technology has made our lives easier in many ways, but at a cost. We are more distracted than ever before, and we are letting our smartphones deactivate the sensors that we all inherently carry with us.

SHARPEN THE AXE

Look around any town or city today and you will notice there are two different groups of people going about their business. The first group is moving to work through train stations and along streets like the walking dead. Their senses are completely shut off from the real world by headphones connected to smartphones, which mean they do not have to make connections with others or pay any attention to changing situations until it is too late. They are passive members of the environment who make no positive or negative contribution to it. They are like animals in a zoo, so far from their natural habitat that they have forgotten what being a wild animal is about. They become creatures of habit, and creatures of habit are by nature lazy and predictable. They are not good at multi-tasking and they lack situational awareness. Under pressure they will start to make mistakes. These people are not using their senses – instead of sharpening the axe, they have left it in a dark shed.

Then there is the second, smaller group. These are the people who pay attention to their surroundings because it matters. Many of these are people with good intentions, such as those who work for the police and emergency services, as well as an increasingly larger group of off-duty service personnel and veterans. These people are protectors but they also pay attention to their surroundings because they don't want to be in the zoo being watched. But there are also people with bad intentions in this group: those people looking for opportunities to exploit and take advantage of the first group. The more we shut ourselves off from our senses, the easier it is for these people to flourish.

Left of bang

Left of bang is a term that was coined by authors Patrick Van Horne and Jason A. Riley to illustrate the concept of deterrence. If 'bang' is the incident or attack, right of bang refers to everything that happens afterwards. Actions right of bang are **reactive**. Left of bang, on the other hand, refers to all actions that are taken before the incident, e.g., using behavioural analysis to identify potential threats, being aware of pre-event indicators, or taking action to interrupt the incident. In short, it is taking the initiative to stop bad things from happening. Actions left of bang are **proactive**.

O.O.D.A.

Developed by military strategist Colonel John Boyd, the O.O.D.A. cycle is a four-step approach to decision-making that describes how the mind deals with its outside environment and translates it to action.

Observe

Observation is not a passive step; it requires an active effort to seek out all the available information by whatever means possible. Our ears pick up sound and we turn to look in the direction of that sound. We start to really observe when we look for patterns. For example, a marine knows that nature has a voice so we learn to listen to it; if you stop and are silent on a walk in the woods you will start to pick out normal patterns and sounds. When those sounds stop, it means there is something out of place. If you stomp through the woods with your headphones on you will not hear it.

Orient

Orientation is how you connect the observed information to figure out what is going on. It involves thinking, doing, memory, culture, upbringing. All of this information works together to form a picture of the situation as you see it. Others in your team may orientate differently because of their experience and background. Orientation gets more difficult when things are complex because you don't have all the resources you need and the picture you have of the situation is incomplete. When this happens, you need to go back to basics and be humble with your decisions.

Decide

Decisions are based on what you think is happening as well as training and experience. Through repetitive training, some decisions can become automatic or reflex.

Act

Action describes the implementation of a decision. A decision is an idea that we are testing, so it's important to observe the results and go back through the process again. In a complicated situation you will make a decision and observe the impact of the decision on the situation almost immediately. In a complex situation your action may add to the situation in ways that you cannot observe or do not expect.

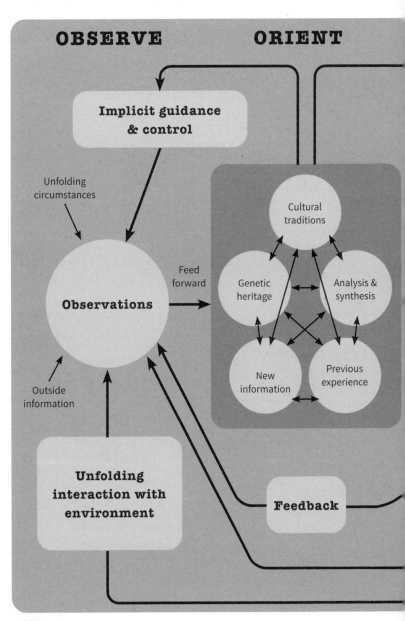

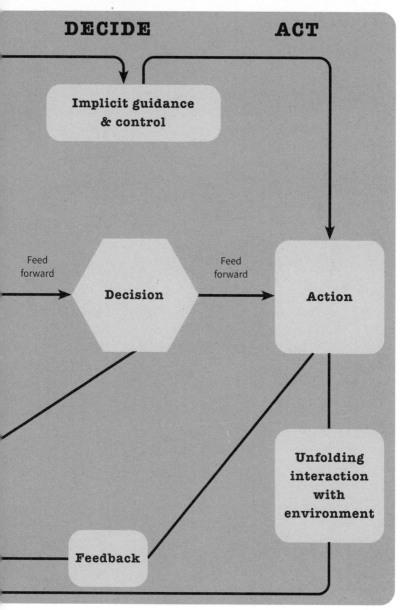

DYNAMIC SITUATIONAL AWARENESS

Marines are constantly reinforcing the sensor sides of our brains with practical tools to improve and sharpen our senses.

Situational awareness can be described using an increasingly popular buzzword: 'mindfulness'. However, this is dynamic, proactive attention, as better situational awareness allows you to take the appropriate action.

The starting point, as ever, is about understanding our own awareness. To do this, let's look at a tool devised by US Marine Lt-Col John Cooper (1920–2006), the awareness colour code chart, or Cooper's Colour Code.

A recent addition has been level BLACK – this is where we become overloaded by the situation and become reactive rather than able to take appropriate and sensible action. It implies panic and lack of control.

WHITE

This is the lowest level. You are switched off and unaware of what is going on around you. You are not ready for anything. Reasons why you may be in this condition include: sleep, fatigue, stress, drug or alcohol use.

YELLOW

You are alert and aware but also calm and relaxed. You are alert to your surroundings and environment, including the people around you and their body language. You are not paranoid, however. You are unlikely to be taken by surprise in this state.

ORANGE

This indicates a heightened level of awareness. You sense that something is not right, so now is the time to evaluate and formulate a plan. Evasion and diffusion works best here (before the next level).

RED

The threat has been verified and the fight is on! You are taking decisive and immediate action.

COLLECTIVE SITUATIONAL AWARENESS

This is what happens when marines work as a team. Collective situational awareness allows us to figure out:

The exact nature of the problem, its cause and any confounding complicating factors.

•

The skills, strengths, weaknesses and experience of their fellow team members.

•

An understanding of what is likely to happen based on taking no action.

•

An understanding of what is likely to happen if the team chooses a specific action.

•

A shared knowledge of the desired outcome.

•

A shared strategy, with an understanding of what tactics need to be accomplished, by whom, and when.

•

The knowledge that any member of the team, regardless of position or experience, can respectfully question the strategy and/or provide additional cues that help the team gain a better understanding of the situation as it unfolds.

USING A BASELINE TO
IDENTIFY ANOMALIES

A baseline is what is normal or expected for the environment, situation or individual. Anomalies are things that should be happening but aren't, or things that are happening but shouldn't. Look at this example of a coffee shop baseline:

Anomalies
things that shouldn't be happening but are

Normal expected activity
- Conversation
- Coffee machines
- Staff moving about
- Tables being cleared
- Door opening and closing

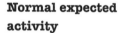

Anomalies
things that should be happening but aren't

In our coffee shop we are having a quiet conversation. We have ordered coffee, but even after 10 minutes it has not arrived. The shop is not too busy so we start paying attention. The door is open. We can hear raised voices outside. There is no one behind the counter. Something is different. These anomalies help us make a decision as to whether we can be useful in this situation and we take action by going and investigating.

THE SIX DISCIPLINES OF BEHAVIOURAL SCIENCE

In order to become more aware of our surroundings we need to think about the ways that information can be relayed. There are six areas to think about and they range from autonomic to deliberate, and personal to social.

Kinesics

This is the study of conscious and sub-conscious body movements and gestures, often referred to as body language (see pages 82–4 for examples).

Biometrics

These are biological responses, such as someone's face or neck going red when they speak about a subject they are anxious about.

Proxemics

We often use this when we arrive at a party; it's looking at space and distance to identify and observe groups who know each other and people who are less comfortable. How and where people stand can tell us a lot.

Geographics

This is about assessing people within an environment. Who is out of place in a railway station or shopping centre? It's about spotting the people who are not doing what we'd expect them to do in specific locations.

Iconology

This is about spotting items of clothing or tattoos or other signs that give us information about someone, whether it's a suit, a smart watch, a tattoo, a piece of jewellery.

Atmospherics

These are the collective attitudes, moods and behaviours in a given situation or place, as well as the general behaviour of a crowd or a mob – you'd see this if people were running away from an incident.

EXAMPLES OF NON-VERBAL COMMUNICATION
[body language]

Leaning away from someone

Indicates we dislike or disagree with them.

Crossed arms

If arms are crossed suddenly this is a sign of discomfort.

Hands on hips
Establishes dominance or
highlights there are 'issues'.

Arms behind back
Keeps people at bay; can indicate
anger or frustration.

Steepling fingers
A powerful display of confidence.

Neck touching
Indicates emotional discomfort,
doubt or insecurity.

Jiggling feet
Indicates discomfort.

Crossed legs
Indicates we are comfortable.

Toe pointing upwards
Suggests a good mood.

PUTTING IT ALL TOGETHER

We use the six disciplines of behavioural science (see page 80) at different times and for different reasons:

To assess individuals – we use kinesics, biometrics and personal iconology.

•

To assess groups – we use proxemics.

•

To assess the environment – we use geographics and environmental iconography.

•

To assess the collective – we use atmospherics.

Consider the following situation:

We arrive at a party. Straight away we see that a group in the corner look like they are having a heated discussion (**kinesics**, **proxemics**). Another pair are whispering (**kinesics**, **proxemics**). In the corner is a man who has a flushed red face and seems to be looking for something (**biometrics**). The groups are all separated and don't seem to know each other well (**proxemics**). The party is in a room that is not big enough for the number of people, it is uncomfortable (**geographics**). A loud group all have the same tie on (**iconography**). There is an undercurrent of aggression rather than fun (**atmospherics**).

This is a perfect example of how we can use all six behavioural science disciplines to assess individuals, groups, the environment and the collective.

HOW TO DESCRIBE SOMEONE TO A POLICE OFFICER

When we pay attention to our surroundings, we can be more useful before, during and after an incident. If we see a suspicious man or woman, we can give an accurate description to the police using the A–H method.

A

Age

E

Elevation (height)

B

Build

F

Face

C

Complexion

G

Gait (the way they walk)

D

Distinguishing marks

H

Hair

HOW TO DESCRIBE VEHICLES TO A POLICE OFFICER

Another way we can be useful is being able to describe cars accurately. When taking down details, police officers will always want to know the following:

Shape

Colour

Registration

Identifying marks

Make and model

'You don't wait until you're in an unexpected storm to discover that you need more strength and endurance. You don't wait until you're on a mountain climb to become a good climber. You prepare with intensity, all the time, so that when conditions turn against you, you can draw from a deep reservoir of strength. And equally, you prepare so that when conditions turn in your favour, you can strike hard.'

Roald Amundsen

Know Your Environment

The foundation of simple survival skills starts at home. Home is a place where you can learn about risk without significant consequences. It is here that you can learn, practise, make mistakes, reflect, adapt and repeat.

Riding a bike, juggling or playing an instrument are all examples of technical skill – the more you practise the better you get. The same applies to survival skills, whether it's lighting a fire, hunting or moving quietly and quickly through woods.

THE FOUR SURVIVAL PRIORITIES

Survival in any environment starts with becoming part of that environment – adapting to it, not fighting it. In a wilderness survival situation, that means becoming like a wild animal. However, modern life has created the conditions where survival is easy. We don't even have to think about what we need to survive:

Hungry?
Go to the fridge for food.

Raining?
Take shelter inside.

Cold?
Turn the fire (or central heating) on.

Thirsty?
Go to the water tap.

What used to be big problems for humans now have simple solutions that require minimal skill or knowledge, which means that basic survival skills seem superfluous. We can go for a long walk in the woods without carrying much because we have food at home. However, when something bad or unexpected happens, simple things that were not important suddenly become crucial.

Food = Fuel

Shelter = Protection

Fire = Heat

Water = Life

So now what? Let's think about what you might need to survive in the wild:

Find a small rucksack or backpack and check the zips and straps are all working and that it will carry about 10 kg. This is your grab bag for any walk from now on. At the very least, you need to carry items that relate to the four survival priorities.

Food

Enough for 24 hours. The food should have a long shelf life: beef jerky, salted almonds, energy bars or flapjacks are really good. A good addition is a squeezy container of honey and some tea bags. Put everything in a freezer bag to waterproof it and then tape the bag with black masking tape.

Shelter

A lightweight tarpaulin that packs small is really handy. Save time and effort by tying each corner with paracord. Add two bungee cords and at least six tent pegs.

Water

Take a good water bottle – there are some excellent metal water bottles available. Water purification tablets are light and cheap, and could save you from becoming ill.

Fire

It is good to have a flint and magnesium, better to have some waterproofed matches, but best to have a good-quality lighter.

You will also need a good sharp knife and a compass. With these basics you will still have room for specific additional items, depending on where you are and what weather you will encounter. What is important is that you now have a survival 'school bag', which means that everywhere you walk from now on can easily become a classroom to practise and experiment. It is not that heavy, and it will make a huge difference to the knowledge you will gain.

A full modern survival kit is not necessary in most situations but if you take the example of someone travelling abroad on a gap year, their kit list might look like this:

Food and Water	**Phone** (and portable charger)	**Extra Dry Clothing**
Survival Blanket	**Shelter**	**Sun Protection** (glasses, sunscreen)
Sanitary Products	**First Aid Kit**	**Cash**
Emergency Credit Card	**Medication**	**Fire**
Knife	**Local Map**	**Compass**
Torch	**Documents** (passport, driving licence)	**Portable Radio**

THINK LIKE THE ICE MAN

When Winston Churchill spoke of the early commandos he said he was looking for the 'hunter class' – independent, competent, self-sufficient. Ötzi the Iceman is the name given to the oldest mummified man ever found intact and tells us a lot about what the earliest man of the hunter class was like. He lived around 5,300 years ago and was discovered by two German hikers in 1991. His body was perfectly preserved in glacial ice, meaning that we are able to understand much about his way of life.

Ötzi was well equipped to master the challenges of his alpine environment. He was adept at hunting with a bow and arrow, dismembering animals with his dagger, fashioning and repairing his equipment and making a fire (his soot-blackened lungs suggest he spent much time close to open fires).

He knew which wood to use to make arrows and how to carve a bow. He used flint tools and a copper axe – both as a weapon and to cut down trees.

His survival equipment gives you a good idea of the essentials that are needed and the technical skill required to operate in the demanding alpine environment.

Copper axe used both as a hunting weapon and to cut down trees.

Longbows, arrows and a quiver

The quiver contained arrows and four deer antler tips – perhaps for skinning animals – and a 2-metre-long piece of string made from tree fibres.

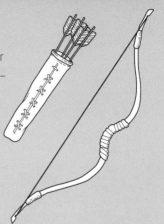

Flint dagger and a tool to sharpen it.

Two containers made from birch bark

The inside of one of these was blackened and contained freshly picked leaves and charcoal fragments, so it can be assumed that Ötzi wrapped charcoal embers in the leaves and carried them with him, enabling him to create a new fire in a matter of seconds.

Backpack made using hazel rods and a sack or net; this would have been used to carry firewood.

Stone disc on a belt used for hunting birds.

Birch fungus that may have had antibacterial qualities but can also be used to carry embers or used as tinder.

BUILD AND LIGHT A FIRE

Learning to build and light a fire in the garden is a great way to practise and repeat a simple skill until you get it right, plus a shared fire unlocks a primal feeling of safety. Building a fire is simple, as long as you follow the rules.

Rule 1
Be patient!

Rule 2
Start by getting everything in the right place.

Rule 3
Decide what the fire is for. Warmth? Cooking food? Boiling water?

Rule 4
Pick the right spot: is it safe, practical, does it allow room for friends?

The Fire Triangle is an easy way to understand the basic ingredients for a fire (Rule 2); if any are missing you'll have problems.

Notes and tips for a successful fire

• Your fire is born the second the tinder takes a spark – you'll hear popping or crackling as the flame takes hold.

• The dry kindling will catch quickly, and you will feel like the first ancient human when they mastered fire.

• Look for signs that the kindling is burning really well before you decide to add more wood, as at this point it could go either way.

• Look for signs of heat – does it feel hot?

This is the air all around us. When you build a fire you need to ensure good airflow, so the oxygen can feed your fire.

This is provided by your flint, matches or lighter.

This is what catches fire: tinder takes the flame and burns hot and fast, kindling holds the flame with enough air to turn the flame into a fire and dry wood builds the fire (but don't add it too soon or you'll destroy the fire).

• Add fuel slowly, starting with smaller pieces and place them carefully. A fire needs airflow.

• Place the larger logs close to the fire and slowly add, these will be the source of heat for the next few hours.

• When you have finished with your fire, always make sure you have extinguished it completely by sprinkling the embers with water. Put your hand near the ashes; if you can still feel heat, it's not out. Apart from being crucial to avoid wildfires, it follows the outdoor principle of 'leave no trace'.

SHELTER

Shelter is important to protect us from the elements, particularly in certain environments. Here are some different ways you can protect yourself.

Snow hole

To build your own snow cave you'll need to look for a substantial snow drift, away from any potential avalanche threat. Start carving out a tunnel in a slightly upward direction. Continue to shape a domed area that will allow you to at least sit up comfortably. The walls should be at least 12 inches thick to provide suitable insulation. Then begin to sculpt an elevated area for a sleeping platform. Finally, create an air vent and build a block to prevent draughts at the entrance.

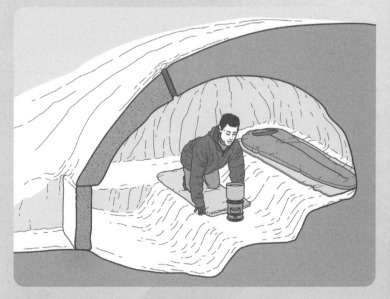

Tarpaulin shelter

With a lightweight tarpaulin, a few tent poles and pegs, and some paracord, you can create a variety of different shelters. Siting your shelter is important – think about wind direction, natural protection from your surroundings, proximity to water, etc.

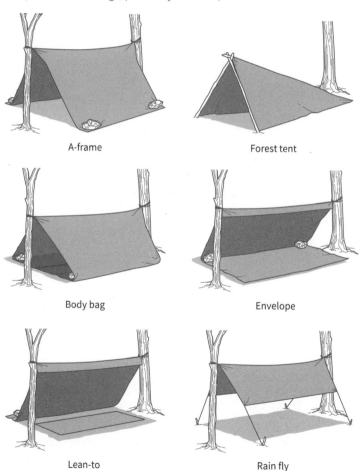

A-frame

Forest tent

Body bag

Envelope

Lean-to

Rain fly

FINDING DIRECTION AND NAVIGATING A COURSE

Marines need to have a good sense of direction, beyond being able to use a map and compass or a GPS device. Every human has an innate ability to find direction and navigate a course without technology. It is knowledge that we have lost, but it can be regained. We all have the potential to use our senses – sight, hearing, smell and touch – to interpret natural signs. We used to use landmarks and features to navigate from A to B; there are many ancient public footpaths and bridleways all over the UK, and when you pay attention you will see that they are often connected by landmarks, such as the edge of a wood, ancient burial mounds or hilltops.

Pathfinding

Marines are often the first ashore so need to be able to navigate effectively. No doubt the easiest way today to find out your location is to use a smartphone, but this system will only last as long as the battery in your phone. It's far better to have a compass and a map, and most sensible people will still use a map and compass when hill walking. It is also useful to learn how to navigate when a compass and map are not available – see this advice from Harold Gatty's book *Finding Your Way Without Map or Compass*:

• **The sun rises in the east and sets in the west. If you can see the sun in the sky you can find north and south.**

• **The best way to learn to find your direction is to walk often and alone. Look for features, landmarks, tracks, vegetation, agriculture, urbanisation, light (natural and man-made).**

- Carry a notebook and write descriptions of what you see and what it means.

- Think in reverse, remember where you have been.

- In each direction you should note the shape of the horizon, the general outline of hills and silhouettes.

- You should be able to navigate effectively on a clear day using observation, with minimal reliance on map or compass.

Visualising a map

When you look at a map you should be able to translate the features on the map into the features you are seeing in front of you. Look at the following examples of how to read contours on a map:

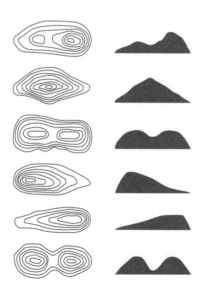

Find direction at night using stars

As long as you have clear skies, you can use the stars to establish the four compass points.

Northern hemisphere

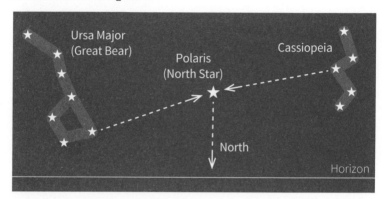

Southern hemisphere

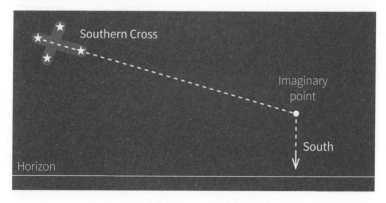

USEFUL KNOTS THAT WILL NEVER LET YOU DOWN

Clove hitch – an essential knot used to start and finish flashing.

Figure-of-eight – a general-purpose stopper knot used to stop ropes from running out of devices.

Bowline – used to make a fixed loop in the end of the line. It is relatively easy to untie when not under load. It is commonly used in sailing small craft.

Distel knot – used to attach a carabiner to a rope, allowing a climber to ascend or descend.

Round turn with two half hitches – used to secure the end of a rope to a fixed object; often used in boating to permanently tie to a mooring.

Fisherman's knot – used to join two lines of equal diameter; can be easily tied with cold, wet hands.

Italian hitch – used as part of a lifeline or belay system with a pear-shaped locking carabiner. The hitch creates friction by having the rope rub on itself and on the object it has been wrapped around. It can be pulled from either side of the rope and is still effective.

Sheet bend – used to join two ropes of unequal size; the thicker rope should be used for the simple bite.

Monkey's fist – this is tied at the end of a rope to serve as a weight, making it easy to throw.

Rolling hitch – used to attach a rope to a rod, pole or other rope.

Reef knot – used to secure a rope or line around an object.

For more information, see *The Ashley Book of Knots* by Clifford W. Ashley.

PUTTING IT INTO PRACTICE

You may have set out to walk a route through the hills to visit a relative, but it has taken an hour longer than normal. Something else might have happened, something may not feel quite right. If the situation has changed, the sooner you recognise this the better.

THINK...

The reasons for this change in situation could be from poor navigation, an accident or a sudden change in weather conditions. Your inbuilt early warning system is critical to the steps you take next.

Early acceptance means that you start to become a creature of your environment rather than an alien fighting against it. As a marine, you are ready for this situation because you have your grab bag with enough food, shelter and water to stay put, or go for help. You are useful and you can start to live *within* the rhythm of nature not *against* it. Your basic kit means that you can start to explore your environment.

- You have 24 hours of emergency rations – this will buy you enough time to focus on finding a good base.

- You have the means to start a fire, which will allow you to cook and boil water to keep clean and warm while you rest.

- You have a lightweight tarpaulin and tent pegs. A good shelter will protect you from the elements.

- You have water and water purification tablets or equipment.

Questions to ask yourself

Whether you are preparing for a trip in the wild or a day in the city,
the questions you need to ask yourself are the same.

How prepared are you for the task
you have set yourself?
Preparation builds self-belief – if the situation changes
how confident are you that you will be OK?

•

How quickly can you switch to a different
approach or strategy?
Flexibility is key.

•

Are you aware of potential problems?
Always anticipate by thinking ahead.

•

Have you thought ahead to potential
challenges, distractions and dangers?
Do you understand the consequences and, more importantly,
what will you do if they happen?

•

Can you give and receive information well?

•

How quickly can you fit into a team?

•

How quickly can you bring new
members into a team?

•

Are you paying attention and observing changes
around you in real time or are you a by-stander?

Achieve

The process of thinking like a marine is all about converting potential into performance – we need to be able to achieve success. All this readiness needs to be put to use. The way to achieve is to find meaning in what you are doing, because then you will know what pride and a sense of self really feels like. You will keep challenging yourself to get better for the rest of your life. This is the final step to thinking like a marine.

Work Together to Aim High

SUCCESS MEANS WORKING TOGETHER

All the lessons up to this point have been about you alone. Now we need to learn how to be part of a team. How to accept new team members and how to find our place in any team that we are joining. Working together makes hard things achievable. (Note: achievable is NOT the same as easy.) In a team, physical strength is just one factor of being a marine. Far more important is mental strength and the simple fact is that good teams make us mentally stronger.

On the battlefield the basic principle is that a marine does not move unless they have another marine in a position to provide covering fire. Marines work together to figure things out. This principle works all the way up to large-scale assaults.

United We Conquer

At a lay-by on the A82 north out of Spean Bridge, Scotland, there is a statue of three Second World War commando soldiers looking south towards Ben Nevis. A plinth near the statue reads: 'In memory of the officers and men of the commandos who died in the Second World War 1939–1945. This country was their training ground.' At the base of the figures are three words: *United We Conquer*.

BE EXPLICIT ABOUT
WHAT GOOD IS

The sense that you are part of something bigger than yourself, that you are in a real team, is hard to describe but you know it when you see it. One word for this is 'cohesion'. Cohesion is the force that acts to unite people. Any action or behaviour that unites the people within a team supports cohesion. Cohesion raises the standards and efforts of every team member. Remember 'United We Conquer'. This is what good looks like. So, ask yourself this question about your team, whether your class at school, your team at work or your sports team: Are we united?

How marines look after their casualties (injured and wounded) is the perfect example of this. It is a simple fact that marines will go forward and do amazing things when they know that they and their families will be supported if something bad happens to them. This contributes to uniting the force and is what we call a moral obligation.

SHARING THE LOAD

When a marine needs help, we share the load. Colonel Charles Vaughan was the Commandant of the Commando Training centre during the Second World War. His philosophy for commando training was that it had to be tough, but there was an underlying ethos of 'sharing the load'. This is part of the reason why there are three commandos on the monument rather than one, and is ultimately the reason for the emphasis on WE in 'United We Conquer'.

BEING A GOOD LEADER

The first principle of leading a team is that it is not about you. Success means 'we' not 'I'. A team leader is part of the team, not separate from it. You don't own, command or control the people in the team; you work with them to achieve shared goals. The badge or title you are given is not a licence to practise your personal idiosyncrasies on other people. The badge or title are there to help you get things done.

A leader makes sure the whole team works together to achieve success.

•

A leader sees potential and works to unlock it, not shut it down.

•

A leader sees through a failure and does not fall into the trap of blaming it on poor character or lack of intelligence.

When a team member fails, the leader fails. This taking responsibility for team members goes from the most junior member of the team to the most senior. Owning it will give you meaning beyond your position or career. You will value it more and use it as an opportunity to pay attention and make a difference to the lives and work of the people you work WITH. If you choose not to own it, then you are failing in your duty to the people you lead and you will damage the team – the larger the team, the greater the damage.

A leader is a catalyst, not an extinguisher

If you ever get the chance to lead a team, the first thing you need to do is build cohesion. You will be given a project or mission or objective to lead the team towards. It could be winning a match or completing an experiment. You then need to collaborate with ALL the team members to get the best result for the team. A leader is the catalyst for the actions and behaviours that UNITE the team. Your words, actions, enthusiasm and energy will cause others to behave in the same way. If you scheme and manipulate and cause division, then the team will scheme, manipulate and divide.

[Division = failure]

WHAT WE WANT IN A TEAM OF MARINES

A sense of mission

A mission gives us meaning and ensures that we have a focus when the going gets difficult.

Morale

Morale is a difficult concept to define, which is why so many people seem to think it doesn't matter. It is the enduring constant attention to the small trivial duties that ensure a person *feels* supported when things get difficult. The foundation of good morale is taking care of the stuff we should not have to worry about, such as pay, reports, basic administration. If someone doesn't get paid, misses a promotion because a report has not been completed or misses a critical course because someone did not stamp the form, the erosion of faith in the organisation begins. If one person is disciplined but another is not, then morale suffers. If you manipulate the system then you erode morale. Low morale stops people doing what needs to be done because they feel it doesn't matter, so if morale is low, look for the divisions and repair them quickly.

Leadership

Leadership means you own the decisions and the consequences of those decisions. You are responsible and accountable when it goes wrong and you get credit for the success. The team is there to help you make the right decision and your behaviour should unite the team.

Harmony

Harmony is the product of mutual trust; it is mutual trust that converts a mob into a cohesive team. Mutual trust allows us to think and act at a higher tempo because we believe in each other.

Teamwork

Marines create and nurture mutual trust by working hard together. Teams that are working hard together develop implicit communication methods. A nod, a raised eyebrow, a pause. A team that trusts each other can read these signs and ultimately it will save their lives.

Esprit

Although the marine, like the group, can be hurt by being pushed beyond sensible limits, their spirit will suffer even more sorely if no real test is put upon their abilities and moral powers. If denied these things, they will come to hold their chief, their job and themselves in contempt. The greater part of a person's satisfactions comes from activity and only a very small remnant comes from passive enjoyment. To keep a marine's spirit alive we need to consider the following:

- They are adults and should not be treated like schoolchildren.

- They have rights; these should be made known to them and, thereafter, respected.

- They have ambition – this must be stirred.

- They believe in fairness – it must be honoured.

- They need comradeship – it must be supplied.

- They have imagination – it must be stimulated.

- They have a sense of personal dignity – it must not be broken down.

- They have pride; it must be satisfied.

> 'To give marines working as a group the feeling of great accomplishment together is the acme of inspired leadership.'
>
> Adapted from: *The Armed Forces Officer*, S. L. A. Marshall, 1950, US Department of Defence

MUTUAL TRUST

Mutual trust encourages individual initiative, which means that when a marine is faced with a problem, they seek out the solution, then take the sensible and appropriate action, without waiting for permission. Mutual trust comes from shared experiences. We have to trust marines to make the right decision under extreme stress. Trust cannot be assumed, and it certainly does not arrive by accident; it is earned through training and working hard together.

Being exposed to demanding yet realistic training scenarios that get increasingly more complex and dangerous is how marines learn to trust each other in battle. This kind of training exposes weaknesses that can be fixed and strengths that can be exploited. There is no better way to build trust in each other than to see each other under the pressure of the real job.

GETTING BETTER

Marines get better by reducing the tiny failures involved in completing any task. This works at an individual level and at a team level. If you want to unleash your potential, then getting better has to be your goal. The marine who is really good at something has simply managed to identify and correct more failures – they still make mistakes but only they notice. The people who fail are the ones who worry about the big stuff and avoid the small stuff. Any challenge is a learning opportunity for a marine, an opportunity to get better. The second a marine feels like they don't need to get better is the second they stop being part of the team. They are only thinking about themselves.

SUCCESS MEANS
MANAGING CONFLICT

Conflict within the team plays a powerful and important role. Conflict produces an emotional response that can sharpen the senses and help team members and leaders develop a curiosity about alternative views. The different experiences of team members and the urgency of the situation profoundly affect the way the team makes decisions. Conflicting viewpoints are a normal part of the decision-making process during a dynamic situation. If conflict is well-managed, it can be a very healthy attribute in teams.

However, if not properly managed, conflict can sabotage the best efforts of any team. People will take sides; views will become entrenched. Blame will be sought by all parties and we will learn the wrong lessons. Poorly managed conflict leads to bickering, scapegoating, confusion, panic, and good marines leaving the organisation.

SUCCESS MEANS HARMONY

If the culture is healthy and embraces open, respectful communication, another significant behaviour is recognised: ready dialogue between all team members, including those who have hierarchical standing within the group. A good team understands conflict, its role in the decision process, and its importance in vetting alternatives. The key is to keep the dialogue respectful and not personalise the differences in opinion.

Effective marines will establish a curiosity about their own behaviour and about the behaviour of their colleagues and their leaders. Instead of simply reacting negatively to comments or suggestions, someone with a healthy curiosity asks:

Why is this person, suggestion or comment upsetting me?

•

What am I holding on to or trying to defend?

•

What is the perspective of my teammate, and why does that person see things differently?

By developing the ability to ask these questions, a marine can depersonalise the conversation and help to develop a shared understanding of the entire situation.

SUCCESS MEANS YOU SET
THE BOUNDARIES

A marine leader will first set the personal standards for their team. They will then demonstrate these standards in all of their dealings with the team. For example:

Operate with an open and curious mind.

•

Communicate well.

•

Be respectful of team members.

•

**Think before speaking –
do you know the facts?**

•

**Honestly admit weaknesses or mistakes –
it's the only way to improve.**

•

Never stop learning.

CLARITY MATTERS

A marine needs clarity. Clarity means that they understand **what** is being asked of them, and they understand **why**. They will then want to achieve success on the task, it will matter to them and they will want to do the job well. A marine leader knows that clarity works better than control. There is a simple reason for this: marines are easier to lead when the leader lets go and allows them to show initiative and realise their potential.

FEEDBACK MATTERS

The degree of respect provided in respectful feedback depends on the make-up of the team, the length of time they have worked together, and their operating environment. Deference to titles and appointments is common in hierarchical systems, but so is the friendly banter often found among marines who feel almost like family members. It is important that leaders of teams set expectations about how they want feedback, and they must address privately any concerns when a team member acts in a manner that shows disrespect. Feedback is a loop; without the two-way element neither party can improve.

Marines work on being explicit with what good looks like. They set the standard and when it is not reached, they find the gap between what happened and what the goal was. Good feedback is about trying to understand why the expected standard was not reached. It is not about blame or character; it is about turning potential into performance, turning a bad outcome into a good outcome.

A SHARED UNDERSTANDING

When teams practise communication techniques that are designed to share understanding, it provides opportunities to build team discipline, broaden the knowledge base of individual marines, and remove hierarchical boundaries to learning. Leaders can establish trust and respect, reduce the chance for error caused by distraction and encourage collective situational awareness. Good leaders encourage team members to understand each other's roles and responsibilities and pay attention to each other's areas of weakness as well as expertise.

HARNESS THE POWER OF DIVERSITY

Marines develop a level of trust that goes beyond technical expertise. They understand the importance of collectively solving problems and value the diversity of opinions within the team. Different backgrounds and experiences mean that each team member has a unique way of viewing problems. Diverse opinions, in any team, lead to some level of conflict. But conflict is not always a bad thing; the success or failure of the team is often down to how the team manages conflict and whether they are able to benefit from identifying differences of opinion. The core value is respect. Every team member, when confronting an idea, action, order or behaviour, must show respect for their fellow team members, regardless of their appointment, position within the team or level of expertise.

Learning to disagree respectfully without being disagreeable is a practical skill. So is accepting critical input without voicing displeasure at the sender of the message. In emergency situations, communication should flow freely, but team members should know where the final decision lies and so should the team leader.

Make Success a Habit

Now that we have a cohesive team, we can start to make them useful in the most demanding environments on the planet.

Desert   Jungle   Mountains

Arctic   Sea   Land

These are places where the weather can kill us as quickly as the enemy. It is not enough to survive in these environments; we are still expected to succeed. In any challenging environment marines need to pay attention to the good habits and drills that we have been taught, as well as the small details, small duties and obligations to each other. If you join a large number of small habitual outcomes together you get one big successful outcome.

FINDING YOUR CODE

Sticking to good habits may not be enough though, because we are operating against a thinking adversarial intelligence. What we need is a code. A code makes the team even stronger under pressure. A code is not a list of values on a poster that people look at as they walk past; a code is part of the force that unites people. It contributes to cohesion and tells you how to behave in adversity and uncertainty.

The only way to truly understand that the code works is to test it. It must reflect the brutal facts of the job that you do. You have to believe in it, but also be able to demonstrate it. The Royal Marines Commandos identified a code or spirit for operating in 1952. It was written by marines who had served in the Second World War and Korea. By 1952 the Royal Marines were the only British military organisation that felt that commando training should continue. They decided that if the country needed useful Royal Marines, then they should be commando-trained, and if the country needed useful commandos, they should be Royal Marines. There was no explicit reference to 'the commando spirit' until this point, so this code is very much the code of the Royal Marines. They had learned some hard lessons, but this is what they came up with:

The Commando Spirit

Morale training is far more important than any other. In particular attention will be paid to:

Determination

•

Enthusiasm and cheerfulness, especially under bad conditions

•

Individual initiative and self-confidence

•

Comradeship

Although provision is made in the course for specific physical tests, it is important that morale training should be continuous and unremitting throughout the course. The men must get the offensive spirit the commando way. Physical tests themselves are an important factor in producing self-confidence and a sense of achievement. The spirit in which they are taken is, however, of supreme importance. It is all in the mind and heart.

Commando Training Instructions, 1952

EMBEDDING YOUR CODE

Having put this code or spirit on paper, the Royal Marines then tested it by developing a demanding and realistic training course where marines had to work together to be successful. The code had to be internalised. Success became a habit. The commando course tests how you apply that spirit – it gives the behaviour meaning. If marines are given values which cannot be tested, they have less meaning. Marines had to see that the four elements mentioned above contributed to success. This means that each element has actions that allow us to see that they are worth doing.

To embed the code, they put marines into challenging situations; when the code was applied the outcome was positive.

Work together.

•

When it gets difficult, work harder together.

•

Follow the code and you will be successful.

LIVING YOUR CODE

At some point after 1952, the Royal Marines shortened the commando spirit to:

Courage • Determination

Unselfishness • Humour in adversity

Marines need a code because they are warriors, meaning they are trained to a high standard in martial skills. This makes them dangerous and dangerous people need a code to protect them. A code is a professional work ethic needed by every professional who has to deal with death, violence and serious injury. There is never a time to take the gloves off in response to an act of terror or an enemy atrocity – when you take the gloves off, you break the code and are no better than the person you choose to take your vengeance upon.

To live your code, you have to make it explicit. It is not enough to write it down and simply say 'this is important'.

A successful code must be achievable.

•

It does not have to be easy.

•

It does not have to fit an acronym.

•

**It should be tested by doing the job,
not by memory or posters.**

•

**A code that works is explicit through what
you do, not what you say you do.**

To test the code, see how it applies to the orientation phase of the O.O.D.A. cycle (see page 72), as orientation is the most important phase and the most difficult to get right.

WHAT DOES A GOOD CODE LOOK LIKE?

The US Army Ranger Regiment has a long and proud history and a direct link to the Royal Marines heritage from the Second World War. The Ranger Regiments trained at Achnacarry, Scotland, prior to D-Day. This is the Ranger Creed:

> **R**ecognising that I volunteered as a Ranger, fully knowing the hazards of my profession, I will always endeavour to uphold the prestige, honour, and high esprit de corps of the Rangers.
>
> **A**cknowledging the fact that a Ranger is a more elite soldier who arrives at the cutting edge of battle by land, sea, or air, I accept the fact that as a Ranger my country expects me to move further, faster and fight harder than any other soldier.
>
> **N**ever shall I fail my comrades. I will always keep myself mentally alert, physically strong and morally straight and I will shoulder more than my share of the task whatever it may be, one hundred percent and then some.
>
> **G**allantly will I show the world that I am a specially selected and well-trained soldier. My courtesy to superior officers, neatness of dress and care of equipment shall set the example for others to follow.
>
> **E**nergetically will I meet the enemies of my country. I shall defeat them on the field of battle for I am better trained and will fight with all my might. Surrender is not a Ranger word. I will never leave a fallen comrade to fall into the hands of the enemy and under no circumstances will I ever embarrass my country.
>
> **R**eadily will I display the intestinal fortitude required to fight on to the Ranger objective and complete the mission though I be the lone survivor.
>
> Rangers lead the way!

Like the Royal Marines Commandos, the US Navy SEAL teams can trace their heritage back to the Second World War. This is the SEAL Ethos:

> In times of war or uncertainty there is a special breed of warrior ready to answer our Nation's call. A common man with uncommon desire to succeed. Forged by adversity, he stands alongside America's finest special operations forces to serve his country, the American people, and protect their way of life. I am that man.
>
> My Trident is a symbol of honor and heritage. Bestowed upon me by the heroes that have gone before, it embodies the trust of those I have sworn to protect. By wearing the Trident I accept the responsibility of my chosen profession and way of life. It is a privilege that I must earn every day.
>
> My loyalty to Country and Team is beyond reproach. I humbly serve as a guardian to my fellow Americans always ready to defend those who are unable to defend themselves. I do not advertise the nature of my work, nor seek recognition for my actions. I voluntarily accept the inherent hazards of my profession, placing the welfare and security of others before my own.
>
> I serve with honor on and off the battlefield. The ability to control my emotions and my actions, regardless of circumstance, sets me apart from other men. Uncompromising integrity is my standard. My character and honor are steadfast. My word is my bond.
>
> We expect to lead and be led. In the absence of orders I will take charge, lead my teammates and accomplish the mission. I lead by example in all situations.
>
> I will never quit. I persevere and thrive on adversity. My Nation expects me to be physically harder and mentally stronger than my enemies. If knocked down, I will get back up, every time. I will draw on every remaining ounce of strength to protect my teammates and to accomplish our mission. I am never out of the fight.
>
> We demand discipline. We expect innovation. The lives of my

teammates and the success of our mission depend on me – my technical skill, tactical proficiency, and attention to detail. My training is never complete.

We train for war and fight to win. I stand ready to bring the full spectrum of combat power to bear in order to achieve my mission and the goals established by my country. The execution of my duties will be swift and violent when required yet guided by the very principles that I serve to defend.

Brave men have fought and died building the proud tradition and feared reputation that I am bound to uphold. In the worst of conditions, the legacy of my teammates steadies my resolve and silently guides my every deed. I will not fail. **"**

We can see from these examples that a personal or group code or creed is designed to be internalised. It is carried by a marine, not on a card in a wallet, but in their actions.

The Royal Marines Commando spirit, the Ranger Creed, the SEAL Code and many other codes are internalised by the individual experience of the different courses, where mutual trust is essential, leading to cohesion and strength in unity. Under pressure the bond gets stronger.

At the heart of these codes is the simple fact that every individual can be relied on to look after themselves. From their bed, to their kit and equipment, to their feet and their fitness. They take ownership of the things that they alone control and are rigorous in their effort and attention to detail. When you can be relied on to look after yourself, then you can be trusted to look after bigger things – a team, a mission, a unit.

Be Reliable

Whenever a marine completes a difficult or demanding course or challenge, there are always those who try to take the credit. Of course, leaders and instructors have a role to play, but ultimately it was the individual or team that decided to work to achieve the goal they were set. If at any point you see an improvement in your own performance as a result of some of the ideas in this book, then the first thing you need to do is make sure you acknowledge what you have achieved.

When you are successful it's important to recognise it, congratulate yourself and then move on to the next challenge. However, it's almost as important to recognise when you have been unsuccessful; in which case don't fall into the trap of blaming the weather, your parents, your childhood, etc. And don't ever say the most dangerous two words in the English language: 'if only…' Look at why things didn't work, take ownership and do better next time.

Being reliable is about applying the basics, being prepared and being consistent in your routines. When all these small routines are in place, you are in a much better position to deal with any crisis. On operations – and quite often in our normal daily lives – it can feel like we are moving from one crisis to another.

A bad leader will use the crisis as an excuse to ignore basic routines, the small aspects of duty and the fundamental obligation to look after their team. They will often use the situation to justify 'robust leadership', which often means they are prepared to violate their code rather than stick to it more closely. Performance will start to trump reliability.

A good leader recognises that the situation itself is not a crisis, but rather that there are critical points where it could go either way. These crisis points are where we need to be humble with our decisions and pay attention to what happens. This is where we become reliable in difficult situations.

WHAT DOES A RELIABLE MARINE DO?

A reliable marine uses their intuition

A marine needs to be capable of making quick 'good enough' decisions with little conscious awareness or effort. This takes practice. More often than not decisions have to be made in challenging situations where:

The situation is confusing and complex.

•

You don't have all the information you need.

•

You don't have all the kit and equipment you need.

•

It is unclear how your actions will affect the bigger picture.

•

The consequences of getting it wrong are the difference between life and death.

Gary Klein is a research psychologist and one of the founders of a technique called naturalistic decision making. He has worked extensively with the US Marines and emergency operators to better understand intuition. His work is vital to how marines can think better. The following diagram is a useful summary of this way of thinking.

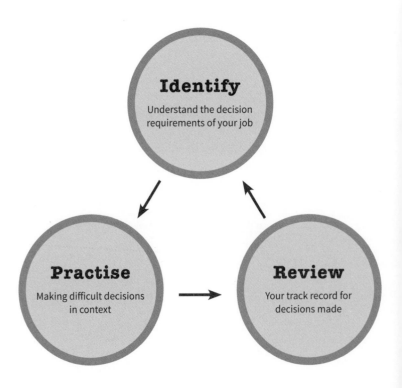

Identify
Understand the decision requirements of your job

Practise
Making difficult decisions in context

Review
Your track record for decisions made

Before you can effectively start to use your intuition, you need to **identify** the decision requirements of your job. These are the judgements that repeatedly arise rather than the one-off situations. To organise your thinking better you can use a decision requirement table (see below). This will help you approach decisions systematically and encourage you to seek out those who have experience of success to get ideas and practices you can copy. By keeping track of your decisions, you can become better at making them.

DECISION

What makes this decision difficult?

What errors are often made?

How do experts handle this better?

Practice increases your experience and you will become better and more skilled at seeing the patterns and building the mental models which underpin your intuition.

Reviewing the decision gives you feedback. Feedback helps you learn from your experiences and become better at making good decisions. Feedback can be time-consuming and painful, but unless you take the time to reflect on each experience you may miss learning opportunities. A debrief can highlight where more practise and training is required so the quality of future sessions is improved.

A reliable marine is a critical thinker

A critical thinker is capable of rapidly processing the information they receive in any form, whether that's details of their physical environment or written and verbal communications. A marine needs to maintain an independence of thought so that they become consistently reliable in difficult situations. This reliability allows a marine to apply good judgement and choose the best option.

There is another important aspect to critical thinking on operations. The ability to recognise your own bias, and understand your own process for making decisions, makes it harder for you to be deceived by your opponent. A marine who is too easily influenced by others, be it with their own team or in their online or digital life, will be easily manipulated by an intelligent adversary. Put another way, it's fine to appreciate and enjoy the skill and expertise of a trained magician, but that doesn't mean you have to believe in magic.

A reliable marine is a creative problem solver

Creative marines are problem solvers – give them a problem and leave them alone. However, when they present their solution to the team it can still be improved. Creative marines are comfortable with failure and accept feedback to achieve the goal (or solve the problem).

'Individuals who are happy to take risks, who are not afraid of failure, who are attracted by the unknown, who are uncomfortable with the status quo are the ones most likely to make creative discoveries.'

Howard Gardner, Professor of Cognition and Education, Harvard University

A reliable marine is self-aware

Self-awareness is the balance of humility (knowledge of your weaknesses) and confidence (knowledge of your strengths). Self-aware individuals are able to regulate their emotions and maintain their ability to learn when a situation becomes challenging. This ability to learn allows them to anticipate problems in advance and predict how they will react to those problems.

The self-aware marine who has learned and anticipated is always ready to adapt in real time.

A reliable marine is socially adept

Socially skilled people have a code of positive values and are able to unite a team. Social skills are the glue that holds a group together. A cohesive team develops social skills through the ability to welcome new members and perhaps – more importantly – to thank those who move on. Social skills are an essential part of how we join a new team or accept new team members into an existing one. These skills include:

Communication

•

Support

•

Challenge

•

Feedback

•

A sense of humour

•

Assertiveness

Of these, assertiveness is perhaps the most commonly emphasised social skill.

Assertiveness
is the ability to exercise
and defend your personal rights,
and to express your needs
opinions and feelings effectively and
appropriately. It also means doing
so in accordance with your personal
values, while respecting the
rights of others and without being
unduly inhibited by worry
or anxiety.

You know you are in a good team when you and everyone else can be assertive. The team gets stronger in the face of adversity. Team members feel they are in control of what matters but also have the freedom to think for themselves and speak up.

A reliable marine is resilient and motivated from within

Resilience has become an overused term. We could look at a marine as being resilient because they have been tested close to breaking point through training. What we are really looking for is the ability to recognise that a situation is challenging, adapt in real time and recover to normal function as quickly as possible. Resilience is therefore the product of the adaptive capacity of the individual. Adaptive capacity has three elements:

The ability to learn, store and use knowledge

•

Creative flexibility on decision making and problem solving

•

Responsiveness

The codes set out in Chapter 8 are not about conformity or being accepted, they are about understanding that when you ALL work together, you can achieve amazing things. It is a choice and an internal desire to improve and engage in an activity for its own sake. The course is not an easy path – there is success and failure along the way – but the journey is worth it. When you rely on someone else to carry you through a course you are not in control of the outcome and the reality is that you will not be ready when a real challenge comes along.

Goals give us something to aim for – the bigger the goal the harder the journey. You don't control the outcome; you can only control the process that gets you there. A goal is a direction not a destination. The process is the small steps along the way that get you to the end. Never change the goal when it gets hard, adapt the process.

A reliable marine has never finished getting better

It is all too easy to complete a training course and then sit back, feeling that your character has been tested and proven correct. There is no requirement to improve. You can stop getting better.

When you choose to *keep* getting better, all failures and successes are temporary because you are learning and, with more time and more practise, improving. You don't define yourself by passing a course or achieving a position; you define yourself by self-improvement.

Along any lasting and meaningful journey, you are bound to fail. Failure helps you learn. If you have not pushed your body to its absolute limits, then you will suffer when you finally reach them.

CONCLUSION

The initial idea behind this book was to show that marines think differently about the problems they encounter. Most of this is down to the fact that they have learned disciplined habits through stressful training. The habits become embedded over time and are an essential aspect of the training they go through.

Despite how it feels at the time, the training starts slowly, with attention focused on the smallest details, from folding clothes to mission-critical personal hygiene. Training for any role, when done well, requires repetition to the point where it can seem laborious. But experts are those that are content to do the repetitive things well. For a marine, all the drills, moves, blocks, the counters, getting your footwork right, learning how to always be in balance – they all matter. On operations or in war, all these moves remain the same, and doing them well matters even more so.

Training to become a marine is about reducing the number of things that can go wrong for the individual first, then the team, then the larger unit. It is not a journey of comfort and ease. The end result is the ability to think differently because you have been pushed to your limit in many different areas, but most importantly you have been given skills and a code that allows you to unite as a team to help others.

The degree of a person's skill is relative to their surroundings, or the challenges they face. The ability to learn throughout your life allows you to constantly update the skills you need and to get better at what you do.

'If it is endurable then endure it. Stop complaining.'

Marcus Aurelius

What I hope this book has shown you is that there are no quick fixes or 'hacks' for marines. It is all about slowing down to speed up.

- We start slow with things like basic hygiene, looking after ourselves and our kit.

- We find a buddy or form a team and we work together to take on harder challenges.

- We set ourselves a big goal that may seem unattainable at times, but we commit to do the work.

- We commit to the present instead of imagining a glorious future.

- We pay attention to what is happening right now, both in terms of the environment and the people around us.

- We understand what it feels like to have a purpose, working hard together as a team.

- We repeatedly ask ourselves 'Can I be better?'

- We create the conditions where people can be useful and work together to achieve success in the most demanding situations.

After about 12 weeks of practice, repetition and determination, we start to speed up.

- We work harder together and suddenly the big goal is achieved.

- We look for the next challenge.

- We set ourselves new goals, whether a qualification, a skill or a business idea.

- We commit to the work.

- We accept the hardship.

- We work together as a team.

- We achieve.

FURTHER READING

From my experience, marines read more widely than a lot of their officers – or at least are happy to admit to it. I have come across too many leaders over the years who would say that they didn't have time to read, and wear that statement like a badge of honour. Mark Twain said that the person who won't read has no advantage over the one who can't read, but I prefer General James Mattis's view: 'Reading is an honor and a gift from a warrior or a historian who – a decade or a thousand decades ago – set aside time to write. Yet many people spurn this gift and still consider themselves educated.'

None of the ideas or principles in this – and many other books – are new. How I have curated and presented them is down to my lifelong enjoyment of reading.

Anticipate

Enchiridion, Epictetus, Dover Thrift Editions, 2004
Learning How to Learn, Barbara Oakley, PhD Terence Sejnowski, PhD, and
    Alistair McConville, Tarcher Perigee, 2018
Make Your Bed, William H. McRaven, Michael Joseph, 2017
Atomic Habits, James Clear, Random House Business, 2018
Getting Things Done, David Allen, Piatkus, 2015
The Stress Effect, Henry L. Thompson, Jossey-Bass, 2010
Happy, Derren Brown, Corgi, 2017

Adapt

The Ashley Book of Knots, Clifford W. Ashley, Faber & Faber, 1993
Finding Your Way Without Map or Compass, Harold Gatty,
    Dover Publications, 2003
The Natural Navigator, Tristan Gooley, Virgin Books, 2011
The Oxygen Advantage, Patrick McKeown, Piatkus, 2015
Natural Born Heroes, Christopher McDougall, Profile Books, 2016
Left of Bang, Patrick Van Horne and Jason A. Riley, Black Irish Entertainment
    LLC, 2014
Boyd, Robert Coram, Back Bay Books, 2004

Raising the Bar, Don Vandergriff, CreateSpace Independent Publishing, 2012
SAS Survival Handbook, John 'Lofty' Wiseman, Collins Gem, 2018
Bushcraft, Ray Mears, Hodder & Stoughton, 2000
We Die Alone, David Howarth, Canongate, 2010
Man's Search for Meaning, Viktor Frankl, Rider, 2004
Stoicism and the Art of Happiness, Donald Robertson, Teach Yourself, 2018

Achieve
The Code of the Warrior, Shannon E. French, Rowman & Littlefield, 2016
The Ill-Made Knight, Christian Cameron, Orion, 2014
The Obstacle is the Way, Ryan Holiday, Profile Books, 2015
A Tactical Ethic, Dick Couch, Naval Institute Press, 2013
Leadership Strategy and Tactics, Jocko Willink, Macmillan, 2020
The Ranger Way, Kris 'Tanto' Paronto, Center Street, 2017
Man Down, Mark Ormrod, Corgi, 2010
The Philosophy of Cognitive Behavioural Therapy, Donald Robertson,
    Routledge, 2019

Please also visit my website **www.thinklikeamarine.com**

Acknowledgements

This book, much like my time in the Royal Marines, was really all about teamwork. The experience of writing a book was completely new to me, so what you are holding in your hands is down to a great team at Pavilion Books: Susan Swalwell, whose enthusiasm remained undiminished and who kept encouraging me with a critical eye; Clare Sayer, who had the most challenging job of editing a first-time author; Geoff Borin, who designed the book's pages; and Peter Liddiard, who turned my fairly rough ideas into some great illustrations.

None of the ideas, concepts or principles in this book are new; they are collected from my own reading over many years. Some are inspired by my time in the Royal Marines, others are from my personal experiences since leaving. They are not necessarily the views of the organisation itself, but I have done my best to paint a picture of the best of the marines I served with. TT and CM are two leaders who continue to serve and have been at the forefront of operations for the last 20 years. They represent what Britain is truly great at.

I am blessed with a very small number of exceptional friends. They know who they are, and I am grateful for their time and support through some challenging periods.

I am grateful to my dad for teaching me how to think, not what to think. A Regimental Sergeant Major in the Scots Guards, he gave me some advice when I joined the Commando Training Centre Royal Marines: 'A wet sink, is a dirty sink.' There is wisdom in that sentence that only those who have gone through room inspections will truly understand.

To my mum Barbara, who as far as I am concerned won her battle with cancer by living far longer than the doctors thought she would. She never complained, despite being in pain day and night. She inspired both the nurses and her fellow patients and, though now gone, is with us every day. She would have loved this book.

Thank you to my brothers, James, David, Iain and their families, who may buy the book before they are given it as a gift.

Thank you to my son Sam for his infectious good humour and to my son Eli for being more excited about this book than anyone else. Thank you to Anne for being a proper Granny.

Finally thank you to my wife Sally, who was there for me when death and serious injury were part of our life. She is the love of my life and the star who helps Sam, Eli, our dog Willow and me navigate our family life.